The Unfolding

"*The Unfolding* is a moving, fresh, unique poetry collection and a generous invitation into the mind of the poet. Both a galvanizing wake-up call and a tender lullaby."

— **Glennon Doyle,** author of the #1 *New York Times* bestseller *Untamed*

"What I love about Arielle's writing is that she takes readers on this journey step by step, filled with wisdom and grace. This book will help anyone seeking to unfold into their bloom."

— **Morgan Harper Nichols,** author of *All Along You Were Blooming* and *Peace Is a Practice*

"Arielle's words are a balm. Somehow, they soothe but also light the fire for growth. That's an achievement."

— **Jedidiah Jenkins,** *New York Times* bestselling author of *To Shake the Sleeping Self* and *Like Streams to the Ocean*

"Perfectly balances the raw, unpolished, guttural feelings with the eloquence and refined beauty of one who has mastered poetry."

— **Propaganda,** author of *Terraform*

"In a voice that is at once gentle and strong, Arielle shows that our process of becoming, while at times uncertain, is as beautiful as a blooming flower."

— **Dr. Hillary L. McBride,** author of *The Wisdom of Your Body*

"Open up to any page and discover inspiration, honesty, and wisdom. *The Unfolding* will leave you feeling uplifted and open to discovering more about yourself."

— **Justina Blakeney,** author of *The New Bohemians* and founder of Jungalow

"If loving and embracing yourself for who you are feels impossible, pick up this book! Arielle invites you to step into your power through her inspiring prose and beautiful reflections."

— **Jenna Kutcher,** *New York Times* bestselling author of *How Are You, Really?*

"Arielle is a sage within our generation, and she's written a guidebook for anyone who has ever felt lost or needed a reminder that breaking is not the end of the story."

— **Hannah Brencher,** author of *Fighting Forward* and *Come Matter Here*

"Arielle gently invites us to explore the uncharted places of our own lives, to face them with courage and vulnerability, and perhaps even discover an unfolding of our own."

— **Jo Saxton,** author of *Ready to Rise*

HarperOne
An Imprint of HarperCollins*Publishers*

The Unfolding

An Invitation to Come Home to Yourself

Arielle Estoria

HarperCollins books may be purchased for educational, business, or sales promotional use. For information, please email the Special Markets Department at SPsales@harpercollins.com.

FIRST EDITION

Designed by Janet Evans-Scanlon

Illustration credits: pp. viii, 43, 58, 73, 100, 117, 134, 162, 174 © Kebon doodle/stock.adobe.com; p. 82 © Alex/stock.adobe.com; pp. ii, iii, 1 © Roni/stock.adobe.com; pp. 31, 137, 143 © artrise/stock.adobe.com; pp. 17, 22, 34, 65, 86, 92, 96,109, 118, 138, 146, 151, 177, 205, 213 © Millaly/stock .adobe.com; p. 125 © C Design Studio/stock.adobe.com; p. 157 © TWINS DESIGN STUDIO/stock.adobe.com; pp. 123, 168, 169 © ysbrandcosijn/stock .adobe.com; p. 99 © katyau/stock.adobe.com

Library of Congress Cataloging-in-Publication Data has been applied for.

ISBN 978-0-06-309442-0

23 24 25 26 27 LBC 5 4 3 2 1

For those whose petals are beginning to unfold,
breathe, and become love.
And for my niece, Amaya: may you learn to
voyage the waters you were made for sooner
and more confidently than I did.

I often hear people say, "I just don't know what to do." I think more often than not, we do know what to do; the cost of our realness just seems too high at the time.

—DEBORAH ADELE, *THE YAMAS & NIYAMAS*

Our deepest fear is not that we are inadequate. Our deepest fear is that we are powerful beyond measure. It is our light, not our darkness that most frightens us. We ask ourselves, "Who am I to be brilliant, gorgeous, talented, fabulous?" Actually, who are you not to be? You are a child of God. Your playing small does not serve the world. There is nothing enlightened about shrinking so that other people won't feel insecure around you. We are all meant to shine, as children do. We were born to make manifest the glory of God that is within us. It's not just in some of us; it's in everyone. And as we let our own light shine, we unconsciously give other people permission to do the same. As we are liberated from our own fear, our presence automatically liberates others.

—MARIANNE WILLIAMSON, *A RETURN TO LOVE*

If I speak in the tongues of men and of angels, but have not love, I am a noisy gong or a clanging cymbal. And if I have prophetic powers, and understand all mysteries and all knowledge, and if I have all faith, so as to remove mountains, but have not love, I am nothing. If I give away all I have, and if I deliver up my body to be burned, but have not love, I gain nothing.

—1 CORINTHIANS 13:1–3, ESV

Contents

An Invitation to the Unfolding

Over the last couple of years, I started to experience a number of substantial shifts in my life. I could feel these shifts stirring, but I didn't entirely know what they meant. In the same year that I made a pact with a few friends to go on dating apps in an attempt to learn the ins and outs of dating, I started a new relationship with a man who would soon become my husband. The bud of that relationship led to opening up parts of myself that I had always known existed, but I didn't know if they would ever get the chance to fully exist. This shift included breaking off relationships as well as attributes and parts of myself that no longer fit the person I was becoming.

I was coming into my own as an artist, and my career was taking off in ways I had never expected. The Christian faith that I had grown up with began to take different forms as I asked questions about how to differentiate and separate the voice of God from authority figures and those close to me. It began to expand into a more inclusive and liberating faith instead of a limiting one that said who could or could not be invited to the table of belonging.

Then came 2020, when everyone's lives came to a halt all at once, when we all noticed the shifting that was happening in not just our individual lives but also our collective one. My husband, John, and I sat in the tension of our canceled wedding plans as the world around us shifted due to a global pandemic and racial reckonings. These reckonings, like for many of my peers, led me to question my identity as a Black Woman and what my value was in this world outside of being a Black Artist or "influencer." I was also still learning how to fully accept and love the glorious being that I am while dismantling cultural and religious assumptions about my body. All while making time to breathe *and* eat. Goodness.

Each of these experiences transformed into important moments that begged my attention and diligence to embrace each one. Each of these moments took shape as different layers within the process of my journey of self-discovery. This process looked like leaving behind the familiar, shedding the comfortable, and embracing the newly revealed parts of myself, which ultimately led to an unfolding and embracing of my fullest self.

Our bodies are constantly in a process of growing, our cells are constantly replenishing, and it's that very cycle that keeps us alive. However, what I've been learning is, it's not just our physical bodies that are constantly changing but also our beliefs, desires, and passions, which shift as we experience love, loss, desire, faith, doubt, conviction, wonder, and everything in between.

Change is a part of life, at the cellular level and beyond. As I worked to make sense of the changes that were happening in my life, I called this lifetime process of growing and expanding "The Unfolding." And this is something every one of us experiences. The process of Unfolding happens over and over again, just like the replenishing of our physical cells. To unfold means to grow, to expand, to peel back the layers of who you've been, unveiling who you will be and stepping into the fullness and wholeness of who you are. There is grieving in The Unfolding, a resenting or longing for what was. There is fear of what is and will be. But most important, there is grace, grit, and miraculous wonder in The Unfolding. It is when you take notice of your wings, your passions and strengths, that you learn to step into freedom and embrace your flight.

I'm a poet, so one of the primary ways I express this Unfolding process is through poetry. The poems in this book were birthed out of my own seasons of hurt and discomfort— from single to engaged, from Baptist pastor's kid to student and explorer of wonder and mystery, from unexplored aspects of faith, from wounded to restored. These poems rose from the ashes of learning that I am not broken and the world I have created around me is not wrong—instead simply Unfolding who I have been all along. My own process of Unfolding has, just like my cells, been renewing and regenerating time and time again, but I didn't necessarily have language for it until now.

Think of The Unfolding process like a glass jar. We all start life with a pristine glass jar, but over time, the jar begins to crack as we learn more about the world and the people in it. Eventually, the jar is too cracked and it falls apart, the pieces shattering all over the floor, and we are left with the decision to either pick up all the pieces and attempt to put them back together as the same jar or use the pieces to create something new. For me, these pieces included my faith and how I viewed God, my upbringing, my ethnicity and race, my relationships with friends and family, and my own voice and existence. These pieces of my life lay on the ground, shattered, but I realized there were still pieces worth picking up and mending with the glue of new perspective and understanding, which brought me back to wholeness, back to God, and ultimately back to myself.

I didn't walk through my Unfolding alone. I had many people whom I would call my guiding songs in the wind. You know those voices of people who can guide you back home, back to yourself, away from the ledge of fear and frantic decisions made because of other, opposing loud voices around you, while the songs in the wind almost whisper, guiding you with leaves and flowers floating in the air (a real "Colors of the Wind" kind of moment). These mentors, peers, friends, and loved ones constantly reminded me that I was okay, that my head was above water, that I had the ability to swim, and that I wasn't going to drown or experience this forever. They helped me see the shore while still (barely) swimming in the middle of the ocean, guided me with truths of who I was and what I was capable of, and reminded me that God was with me, until I could feel my feet on land again.

Throughout these pages, I will take you along this journey of my Unfolding. Each of the following poems, essays, and quotes depict the shedding of my own cells, of past beliefs, the releasing of some parts of what I was raised to believe in, in order to embrace what I believe today. As humans, the greatest capacity we have, outside of being able to love, is to feel, and to feel deeply. To take the moments of hurt and transform them into poem, song, talk, or lesson, passing them on so they serve as a key to unlock healing for others. Read these words while reflecting on what the seasons of Unfolding have looked like in *your* life.

I want this book to be exactly that for you—a moment to exhale, a moment of solidarity no matter how different your background may seem to be, a key to unlocking healing, and permission and grace for your own Unfolding. These words invite you into my process: how I moved from angst and anxiety to confusion and wonder, to creative expression, and, ultimately, to personal acceptance and peace. My hope is that as you read my words, you will be guided through this process and find your own personal acceptance and peace.

The Five Phases

The process of Unfolding involves five phases, which we'll explore in these pages. I call them: The Awakening, The Eclipsing, The Mending, The Illuminating, and The Returning. These five stages are meant to guide and provide clarity for your Unfolding growth process. I'll explain them briefly so you know what to expect as we move through the book.

THE AWAKENING is the initial realization that either things within yourself must change in order for you to step into the next phase of becoming, or the change has already been taking place and you are just now becoming aware of it. The

Awakening shows you the shattered pieces in your life and gives you room to process what needs to remain and what needs to be let go, which pieces to leave behind and which to turn into a new creation, for you to make space for what will be. It is in the process of Awakening that I felt myself tuning in and listening to a soft purr that became a roar within myself, and embracing that lioness self.

Within The Awakening, I found myself holding pieces of who I was, who I thought I had to be, what I had thought I had to feel, and what I was expected to think, and I saw these pieces no longer serving where I was going or who I was becoming. In a sense, The Awakening could be a sort of death of the pieces of a past self you no longer need to carry with you. In The Awakening you must ask yourself: *Am I going to stay the same, or am I going to lean into the change that's beckoning me?* The Awakening can be that moment when it feels as though you are in tune with a new awareness in yourself and the world around you, and once you see it, you cannot unsee it.

THE ECLIPSING is the moment after you have become aware of the shattered pieces. The Eclipsing can feel dark, confusing, and disorienting. It is where you have to sit with your broken pieces, the hurt and confusion, and decide how and what comes with you into the next phase. NASA describes an eclipse occurring when "one heavenly body such as a moon or planet moves into the shadow of another heavenly body."[1] For me personally, this shadowed season was the crossing

---

1 Brandi Bernoskie and Denise Miller, "What Is an Eclipse?" *NASA Knows!* (series), NASA, May 3, 2017, https://www.nasa.gov/audience/forstudents/5-8/features /nasa-knows/what-is-an-eclipse-58.

over of my present self and my future self. These two celestial existences were both of my selves crossing in the same space, but in order to live full, free, and whole, one of them had to pass and be released for the light of who I was becoming to fully exist.

The Eclipsing journey for me was one of sleepless nights, heavy anxiety, and panic attacks in my car. I was overwhelmed. I felt small. I couldn't hear my own thoughts, but even when I could, I felt I couldn't trust them. Weeks upon weeks of interventions with family and friends who felt the need to reroute or bring me back to myself, or back to a Jesus that I had never even left. This was a hard season, and while I wished that every moment could be made easier, I honor and acknowledge that it was still a very important part of the process.

THE MENDING is exactly how it sounds—the process in which you have collected the pieces of who you were and begin to mend them back together into who you will be. This is a conversation of growth, of acceptance, of watching the broken pieces make something new. The Mending is also the season of asking yourself the questions "What do I need for healing?" and "What is keeping me from wholeness and freedom, and how can I face those barriers?" The Mending is a space of forgiveness and, in some cases, of creating and establishing forgiveness even when it isn't being offered by others. It also includes the process of forgiving yourself for what you didn't know before, finding grace in the ebbs and flows and unknowns.

The Mending, though beautiful, can still be messy. Residual hurt may come up, which you'll need to process through, and it won't be all rainbows and butterflies, but it will be healing. My Mending process meant that instead of fighting the changes happening in my faith and trying to resort back to what I knew, I allowed myself to embrace the expansion. That it was okay if my spirituality, my relationship with God, looked different than it had when I was in my teenage years or even my twenties. That my relationship with my husband was still a worthy and loving partnership even if it wasn't what others might have wanted for me. That my career and calling could still be aligned even while shifting. The Mending can also be a season of embracing the newness and releasing the old.

THE ILLUMINATING is the phase when you let light into your newly mended self. It includes the aha moments. It's when other people's opinions of who you are dim into the shadows and your own desires and thoughts come to the forefront of your mind. It's when you become aware of your shoulds and should nots, and can release them because they no longer serve where you are going or who you are becoming. In this chapter there will be the same rhythm of essays, poems, and prompts, but this phase will also include invitations for breath work and simple meditations, so that you can truly be liberated from things that restrain you, and ultimately find release and the permission to return.

After you read about my own Illuminating process, I hope that it shines light on your own moments of aha, that you are able to find yourself and your story in the realizations, and that you can release what no longer serves who you are or who you are becoming. The Illuminating can be such an exhaling process as much as it can be an overwhelming one because you are seeing and realizing what you may not have seen or realized before. Be gracious with yourself here. Sometimes shining a light can also bring up moments of disorientation, hurt, or maybe even anger. Let the light shine on all of that and be tender as you shift through the beams of each one.

THE RETURNING is the final breath of your journey. You have cleared your shadows and your hurts, you have mended and restored, and now finally you can return to yourself. I say "return" because I have found that as we grow and unfold, we are unraveling and peeling back the layers, revealing who we've always been and finally find the space and permission to be.

My journey of Returning was an exhaled awareness that I was and have always been exactly who I needed to be. Even when I was being told in various ways how "far" I was from who and where others wanted me to be, I was able to return to the truth: who I was and who I am is enough, and who I will become will also be enough. The Returning is not an ending, because the journey is truly never over, but for a moment you will reach a resolve, a chapter closing, and in that closing there is a moment in the mirror that releases the response of "Oh, there I am and there I have always been."

It's important to note at this point that nothing is truly linear—not healing, not time, not existing or thinking. So when you sit with these phases, remember that they are not step-by-step ways of thinking. Rather, to experience them is more like how all good Black aunties and mamas cook: you will taste as you go, adding what you feel is missing, and don't even bother asking for a recipe because it's pretty much just heart and soul, baby. You have to listen to your own heart and soul and trust that you know best. When I entered The Illuminating season, The Eclipsing season still felt as though it was close to breaking me, The Mending season still felt just as wonky and messy as The Eclipsing, and in a way, The Returning felt like another Awakening, until there I was again at the beginning of it all. But no matter how much the phases overlapped in my life, or how nonlinear they were, little leaks of light always slipped through the pieces. In each of these phases, I ultimately came to terms with the realization that life is not black or white. The Illuminating phase shows you that maybe there aren't only two paths, maybe there's a third way and maybe there's a light to guide you through it.

Use This Book as Your Guide

I can't wait for you to go on this journey with me. I've purposely created space in this book for you to interact with it—write in it, or at the least grab a journal or some paper to tuck into the pages of this book and write down your thoughts.

There are meditations in the last few chapters. If you have time, sit with them and spend a few minutes breathing and connecting with your inner self. At the end of each chapter, I will leave you with an opportunity to reflect. I hope these questions are just the beginning as you explore and engage with your own process of Unfolding. I want this book to be your bedside favorite that you pick up before you meet the day, giving you the pep talk you need to feel empowered. I hope it's the book you carry with you to motivate yourself and keep your spirits high, or the book you read at the day's end to calm your anxious mind. I hope it's the book that you come back to time and time again, in all seasons of life, as the love letter that reminds you of who you are.

Ultimately, my hope is that these words and experiences bring you back to yourself. When you've finished reading, acknowledge how you too have awakened in your own ways; encountered your own dark, shadow season; mended pieces of who you were and who you are to step toward who you will become; and let the light in time and time again. Remind yourself of your luminescence and how you've returned to your goodness with every single breath.

May these words meet you in your own Unfolding or on the precipice of it. May they be a reassuring whisper that you are right where you need to be, that you can trust your next steps and the guiding voice inside of you.

In order to let something in,

you have to let some things go

In order to heal, you must hurt

In order to grow, you will experience discomfort

and all of this is to make more room for hope

less room for perfectionism and more room for simply being

less room for answers,

more room for questions with integrity

for mystery and wonder that leads you somewhere new

not right or wrong, good or bad

This is The Unfolding

The Awakening

sat on my therapist's semi-comfortable couch, staring out the window as I often did when she asked me a question, mentally leaving the room for a moment to find an answer. "I feel like there's a me that's just watching myself physically live and exist but it feels disconnected. I don't know if I'm fully here or falling apart," I told her, still staring out the window. We had spent many sessions trying to dismantle the anxiety I carried about who I was becoming and the journey of shifting I could feel myself beginning and how that growth was creating tension with friends and family. I felt as though there was a part of me that had awoken in the last few years. I wasn't sure if that person was still me or, even deeper, if I was allowed to unfold into this person.

As I talked through what I now believed, and how I had always more or less held these beliefs, my therapist asked, "So what is truly so different about who you are today from who you've been before?" I had been hearing so many negative responses from loved ones about how much I had "changed" in the last year or so, and how it was "off" from who I was "supposed to be" that I had started to actually believe them. But her question made me aware that I wasn't becoming someone entirely new but rather finally feeling the freedom to step into who I always had been.

I once had a mentor ask me if I was going to live a life that was based on not disappointing people or one that I felt proud of and called to. This question shifted everything for me because I had realized up until that point I *had* been mostly living a life based on not disappointing other people, and I was just now coming to terms with how, in reality, we will always disappoint someone (or a lot of someones), or even ourselves sometimes, so we might as well acknowledge and adjust to that tension. The beginning of my Awakening was realizing that I couldn't live my full life if I did it based on the applause (or lack thereof) from other people.

In the process of Unfolding, I call the first step The Awakening—your initial realization that things must change, *you must change*, in order to step into the next phase of becoming. I'm sure you've had a moment in your life when you stood at a crossroads and realized everything was about to change. This step is about listening to those awakened parts of you and asking, *Is there something here? Is there a person inside who I've been pushing away because they didn't meet the status quo of a perfect* daughter, caretaker, professional? (My own personal descriptors included "Christian," "pastor's daughter," "speaker," "poet," "artist," and "role model.") *Is there a boldness waiting to be unleashed because it doesn't fit with how I've been taught to be?* The Awakening shatters who you have been or have tried to be, what you have believed, and where you thought you were going. For me, it looked like shattering the certainty of the life I'd been leading as I entered into something more beautiful and mysterious than I could see at that point. The Awakening is also when sleeping parts of who you've always been rise to the surface and demand that you either abandon or become them. Pushing them down or ignoring them is no longer an option.

Growing up as a Baptist pastor's kid and the oldest child, I was reminded constantly that I was a leader, and I was expected to live my life as a good example to other people. I followed the rules. I believed in a fear-driven concept of God, and that a life of faith was only allowed to look one way. I believed there could be certainty to everything, answers to all the questions, if I just read my Bible and did what I was told.

During my junior year of college, I co-published a book of poetry with a friend who was the exact opposite of me—where I followed the rules, he was edgy; where I avoided doubt and questions, he wasn't afraid to ask all the questions. He terrified me. I didn't like rocking the boat because that would mean upsetting people. I didn't like being edgy because it drew too much attention. I didn't like poking at certainty because that might make me question it. Our book, *Vagabonds and Zealots*, perfectly described each of us. He was a wandering traveler in both the physical and spiritual senses, with no desire to be tethered to any type of conditioning, and he put a mirror up to anything inauthentic. Me, I was a true zealot of uncompromising pursuit of the beliefs I had been taught and raised in.

◆

That book was the beginning of the breaking—or my awakening, depending on who's looking at it and from what angle. It was the beginning of my exploration, of secretly asking questions about everything I held certain. This was the beginning of me making decisions and knowing deeply in my existence that they were the next *yes* for me, even when the people I trusted opposed these decisions. My "vagabond" friend shattered my conceptions of what it looked like to be a person of faith. Conversations with him shook up who I was and what I believed, how I interacted with other people, and how I created art. In this specific season of my Awakening, I found myself being very aware of what I *actually* believed versus what I had been told to believe. I found myself not being able to reconcile my lived experiences, relationships, and decisions with my former way of thinking. Awakening is not a onetime thing but rather constantly happening, in varying seasons, begging you to pay attention to it and what it's trying to teach you or awaken you to.

Maybe you too have had moments when you started to question what you thought you knew. Oftentimes when we find ourselves met with uncertainty, we position ourselves in fight-or-flight mode, but what if you listened to the humming, what if you followed the dancing light instead? What if it didn't have to be fight or flight but wonder, but acceptance, but following, just to see where the path goes without fear? Maybe you're in that space now. No matter how uncertain you feel, no matter how painful the shattering might be, know that The Awakening now is making space for what will be. And that is a beautiful thing.

◆

PERHAPS THE PROCESS OF **becoming** FIRST BEGINS WITH THE ACKNOWLEDGING OF BEING. WHO HAVE I BEEN? WHO AM I BEING? AND WHO DO I WANT to become?

ARISE

I thought I was crazy,
I thought my tears were blinded weakness,
that my feelings were distracted foolishness
that I could not trust the voice inside of me, whispering,
beckoning me into the uncharted unknown that was
    deemed ungodly,
this was not a breaking,
though there was a bending occurring
this was a reckoning, an Awakening
I found the Divine in the brokenness
in the evenings when I sobbed myself to sleep,
asking for clarity,
begging to be shown something maybe I couldn't see
I was not crazy,
the stirring in my chest guiding what came next
my tears, not blinding me
but clearing a perspective that was no longer mine
this voice, no longer buried inside
led me here to this love,
this wild and beautiful life
this was no insanity,
this was an Awakening

ARTIST

I don't just want to make art

I want to pull our fear of going deeply

within ourselves

and those around us,

out of our soil like weeds

I want to transform spaces,

transcend heaven on Earth as it is

I don't want to just throw words together

and make them pretty,

I want them to remind us

that even the ugliest parts of our story

are still part of the masterpiece

that we look at these broken glass mosaics,

find them worthy

and every bit of what makes us human

I am bleeding through prose

lightning striking through

then and now

here and there

heaven is now

on Earth as it is right now

in this moment

when's the last time you let yourself be in a moment?

deep dived into nothing but the present?

I make art,

I string symphonies in word form

for heaven to be . . .

right here

right

h

e

r

e

so let the veil be torn

let the feelings flood

may you find yourself more human

more mosaic than broken pieces

more stained glass

with the light streaming in

GOD OF QUESTIONS

something like the art of letting go
of everything you've been told once before,
about who to be and who not to be
about who God is and how God speaks
where God shows up and where God does not
the unwinding of religion
and the reuniting of relationship
God resides in the questions
God rests in the waves
God is found in the chaos and yet only shows up as peace
not afraid of your uncertainty or your question marks
meets you in the sandbox of your curiosity
plays with the fragments of familiarity
and when you ask God: *why?*
God tosses it right back: *Well, what do you think?*
listens intentionally
then tells you the story about the art of letting go
of everything you have been told before
to find just who God is and how God speaks
gifting the questions right back to you:
my Beloved, what do you think?

YOU ARE NOT CRAZY FOR HAVING A CHANGE OF BELIEF. You are human & CURIOUS & EXPANDING.

ALL ALONG

a woman can be all things

both bright and bold

flickering radiance and stark beauty

daring and soft

wild and steady

quiet and audacious

able to pave the way of courage for herself

and the women to come after

piercing through generations of fear

I stand out because I was made to

not because I have to

or because it's the pleasing thing to do

there is a riot rumbling in these bones

I have always been a roaring lioness

caged inside

not captive but resting

waiting

this is her unfolding

this is her escaping from the den

there is a rising

happening now

happening here

all along,

all along

Lioness

I loved my husband from the moment I set eyes on him.

Oftentimes people will ask me how I knew that John was my "person." I tell them that something cracked open in me when he entered my life. That the moment our eyes met, I said, "Oh shoot" (well, not that word exactly, but your imagination can fill it in), and in my mind, my heart, my whole being, I knew he was going to turn my world around in ways I couldn't even fathom yet my whole heart was eager for. There is a part of me that I truly feel could not have begun to breathe or be until I met John. It was as though for more than twenty years there was a part of who I was meant to be that had been holding its breath, waiting for the opportune moment to exhale, exist, and unfold.

Before I met John, I was quietly unraveling old mindsets, shifting out of perspectives and actions. I was privately peeling off the layers of assumptions, shoulds and should nots, and exploring what it would look like to allow this next divinely guided season to completely wreck everything I'd known to be true. Lalah Delia, a beautiful soul, author, and writer, says, "The wrong relationships put us to sleep. The right ones, awaken us."[1] This is every bit of what I felt when I met John. There was a lioness inside of me who had always been there (the name Arielle literally means "lion of God"), but I didn't really feel her fully awaken until I met John. This is not to say I met a man and my whole life and existence made sense for the first time, but

---

1 Lalah Delia (@LalahDelia), "The wrong relationships put us to sleep. The right ones, awaken us," Twitter, December 1, 2020, 4:49 p.m., https://twitter.com/lalahdelia/status/1333936372915191809?lang=en.

this pivotal moment gave me breathing room to experience my full self, and for that I am forever grateful.

What John unleashed in me was the permission to explore. Growing up as a pastor's kid, deeply involved in church spaces, there wasn't always room to explore freely. Yes, I was encouraged to listen to God's beckoning, guiding, and leading, but only if that beckoning led to a lifestyle that looked a certain way. When we started dating, John wasn't attending church, which created many arguments between us because I had been taught that if we were going to be a good, wholesome, Christian couple, then going to church was a prerequisite . . . right? That our outward expression of scripture passages in our Instagram bios and mornings at a coffee shop, noses deep in our Bibles, that these spectacle-based aspects of being a Christian, were necessary check marks for what a healthy Christian relationship leading to marriage was supposed to look like.

Looking back, I can see how much of my life was tied up in the knots of feeling like I "should" act or be a certain way, and that "should" was dictated by other people. One of those guiding voices I mentioned before once asked, "What do you *want* to do or be?" Then said that it was okay if the answer was not what others thought you should do or be. I am *still* wrestling with this one. These external expectations can leave you anxious and sometimes unaware of your own conscious thoughts or decisions, because all you can think about is what you *should* be doing, who you *should* be in this world. But the reality of your existence has never been about who you *should* be but about embracing who you are and finding the wonder and grace of a God who does not "should on you."

My own shaping involved setting necessary and healthy boundaries when it came to making life decisions for myself and not for the sheer motivational applause of others. I stopped going through the motions at church and instead found church communities where I felt I could ask questions and explore my faith, and where I could contribute my unique gifts. And I stepped out of spiritual spaces that weren't inclusive or inviting and toward the LGBTQ+ community. I grew more intentional with what I was saying yes to in my professional and personal lives. I spent time unraveling a lot of what I had grown up to believe about God and religious traditions and learning to interpret holy scriptures in new and expansive ways. I recognized that I desired an egalitarian relationship in which my voice as a woman was valid and my gift of feeling deeply was not used as a reason to discount or diminish my presence.

And I know this shaping is not finished. If it was, then life would be over, wouldn't it?

Sometimes this process of Unfolding begs our whole attention, urges us to lean into the discomfort, embrace the unfamiliar and yet longed for exhale. The whole time I dated John, I felt as if I was holding my breath a little bit, as if I couldn't fully allow myself to fall into the freedom of just being—of being my full self, of being fully loved and loving in return. When I finally did release that exhale, it was such a beautiful release; what initially had been just a stirring was now a full-on awakened roar. Now I truly feel as if I have become my name—that I have become this bold, audacious woman who knows exactly who she is and walks like it. An unlocked purr turned into a tenacious roar that revealed not just the strength

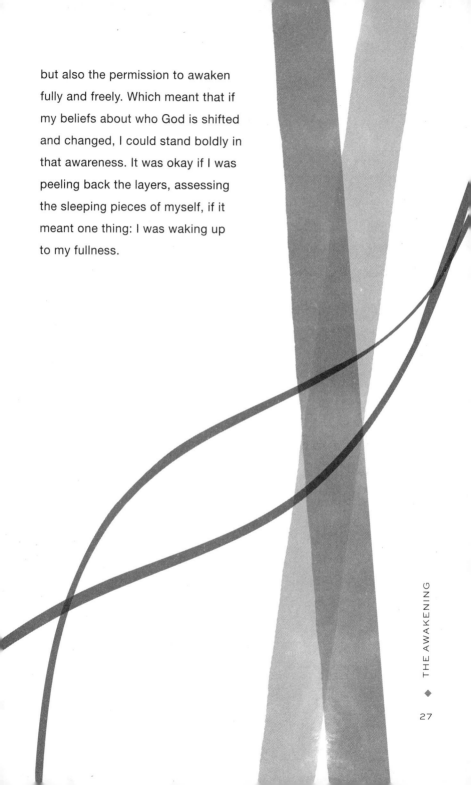

but also the permission to awaken fully and freely. Which meant that if my beliefs about who God is shifted and changed, I could stand boldly in that awareness. It was okay if I was peeling back the layers, assessing the sleeping pieces of myself, if it meant one thing: I was waking up to my fullness.

WAKING

who told you

that the lioness in your chest

was distraction

when she has always been a reminder?

who told you that the roar was a hum,

a sound to be ignored?

who told you to deny your beckoning?

who whispered that your purpose was a misstep,

assumed the path your feet paved

was confusion of direction and not trailblazing

keep winding

keep listening

this is no episode of bewilderment

you are not confused

you are the most sane you have ever been

and this, this moment right here,

is the most awake you have ever felt

EVEN STILL

when there is no longer life in my being

when my breath has fallen short

and there is no blood pumping in my veins

when my mouth no longer has enough

language on my tongue to express

I just want to be remembered like sunflowers

how versatile they are

how their seeds can be both food and oil

how they are more than just pretty things to see

or pluck

when I'm gone, tell those wondering about the remains of me,

that words fell from my palms like sunflower seeds

tell them that I stood as tall as willow trees

that I was more old soul than I was millennial

tell them that I danced like everyone was watching

that I was Bay Area overcast and Southern California sun

tell them I loved like there was a no vacancy sign

placed over my heart, where the light was always broken

and flickering

that there was always room even when all the beds were filled

when there is no longer breath in my lungs,

or a heart making music within my rib cage,

tell them I carried a lioness in my shoulders

and helped other women hear their own roar

tell them I loved the way a wave loves a shore,

always coming back, never fully letting go

tell them I carried more hearts and stories in my hands

that my imprints are threads of everyone I've ever met

tell them that I am still pieces of them even when I'm no

longer here

tell them I was a poem

that each breath,

every smile, was a metaphor

tell them to never forget me

light a candle on my birthday

to let my soul remember what Earth felt like again

tell them I was laughter

the kind that follows you all day—

the kind that creeps back into conversation unexpectedly

the kind of laughter you have while at church and the pastor

is speaking

and you shouldn't be laughing but you can't help it—

wild and uncontrolled

tell them I thought I was everything wild and uncontrolled

that I wanted to be wild and uncontrolled,

mysterious and exciting

yet all I knew how to be was

safe and inviting

and that was okay too

show them how I poured myself into this art

◆

how I let it become me

tell them to sing at my funeral,

tell them to dance when they bury me,

to sprinkle sunflowers over my casket

and when time passes,

return every once in a while just to tell onlookers

that even still, beautiful things grow here

I FEEL LIKE

I feel like a bird who has just learned that she has wings
who has barely grasped the fact that she is not limited to
    the ground
but has more space to expand than she knew
I feel like a dam, where the walls have crumbled to the ground
and the water finally has permission to go wherever it
    wants to
I feel like a waterfall after winter
no longer frozen but free and flowing
effortless in its ability to simply do what it was made to do
I feel like a sunset, anxiously waiting for its turn to paint
    the sky
to splash colors across the horizon in whatever way it desires
to show the world:
look at what I was made to do,
make beautiful things on purpose
and look who I was made to be,
be a beautiful thing
on purpose

THE NOISE

They can say all they want
They can shout all their fears
They can throw doubt
in a space of uncertainty
time and time again
but good thing I know who I am
good thing I know who I am
good thing I know

I WILL NOT BE AFRAID OF *my growth,* EVEN IF OTHERS ARE AFRAID OF IT FOR ME. THEIR FEAR IS NOT MY FEAR. THEIR FEAR *is not my fear.*

We Are Worthy

The church my parents took over as pastors was considered a "dying" church—not many new members were coming into the space, the church didn't really have the means to engage with the community around it, and the pews had stayed as they were when the church was first built. Physically and spiritually, the church and the people within it were fading. My parents, being young and filled with passion, doing their best to listen to the heartbeat of the times, began engaging with the community, reaching out to nonprofits and other organizations to set up summer programs and holiday festivals, connecting with local shelters for the unhoused and doing their best to give people a safe space, a home. Strides were made, but for a Baptist traditionalist church, some traditions remained the same.

Though I grew up with both my parents being equally involved in ministry, there were different names for their roles. For instance, where one was a pastor (my dad), the other was a teacher (my mom, even though equally ordained). But no matter the titles or the stage she found herself on, my wise, discerning, and equipped mother always had a voice and used it powerfully. In an attempt to engage with the younger community, we had a service during which one of the young boys preached a sermon, suit and tie and all, from the pulpit. Weeks later, my mother was scheduled to preach for Mother's Day but was *advised* to speak on the floor, at eye level with everyone else. This stifling of women's voices is one of the reasons I no longer identify as Baptist. And more and more I came to find in evangelical- and Christian-identified spaces that it was not only women's voices but also women's bodies that were regulated and ridiculed, their humanity constantly abused, misused, or completely ignored.

For generations, patriarchal society has told women that we can't trust ourselves, our bodies or our minds. In Christian contexts, this stems from the example of Eve and how she is faulted as the cause of the entire downfall of humanity because of a bite of fruit, or in Greek mythology how Pandora's Box released all the evil into the world. And the common denominator is that these stories are not being told by us but about us. We are told that we—our thoughts, our actions, our decisions—are selfish, sometimes even "unholy" or absent of the Divine, and we tirelessly find ourselves in places where our worth is less than that of men. Especially when it comes to being a Black Woman, universally known to be borderline invisible until noticed for being angry or loud or viewed as just too much. We are repeatedly being told that we don't belong "up there" on the stage, with the microphone, with the higher salary, in the White House, with a voice worth listening to, in positions of power, when we have always been just as powerful, just as enough and worthy of receiving.

Over the years, I have found moments in my life when I could be on stage and express myself but would be asked where my husband was and how long he was going to "allow" me to be so opinionated, so outspoken, so *bold*. I remember attending a church conference where one of the pastors came up to the booth I was working at and asked me if I "thought God had made a mistake." Not knowing what in the world he was talking about, I responded with a nervous chuckle and

THE UNFOLDING

◆

36

asked, "What do you mean?" He pointed to my nose piercing and, in all seriousness, said that I must have thought God had made a mistake when creating me, otherwise I wouldn't have done that to my face. As if this was not my body that I was completely permitted to do with what I wanted. I shrugged off these comments, but you can see they have stuck with me all these years.

Later, I attended an event celebrating and providing soul and self-care for Black Women in the community, and the organizer, Dr. Melina Abdullah, shared how the event came to be. She had thought about the space she wanted to create and how and who it would be for, and she shared how big and crazy the whole thing felt, then followed up with "We [Black Women] need to stop believing that we're crazy for hearing from God. We are divine too. We are worth being spoken to and spoken through." I offer that back to you. For all the moments you've frantically sought out mentors, teachers, gurus, or coaches in hopes that they would tell you what you already knew. For the nights that you tossed and turned in indecisiveness that was not your own because you were made to question or doubt your own voice, your own guiding, your own wisdom. For all the times your authenticity or authority was questioned. Not only are you worth being spoken to and spoken through but also you are equipped to do the speaking.

This is where The Awakening comes into play. It allows you to become aware of your ability to trust yourself and your decisions. To walk confidently in your Divine Authority. To awaken to the fact that unlike what you've been taught to believe, choosing yourself, choosing what feels best for you in that next moment, not only sets you on the path you're meant to be on but also that bold audacity sets up the freedom for others. Imagine that when you say yes, when you take that next step toward claiming and owning your voice, your body, and your choices, you crack open the doors for others to do so as well. This lioness inside reminded me that I can trust myself and my decisions. You are not selfish, unholy, or unworthy. You are awake to your potential, and to that potential opening up opportunities for others to learn and grow. If there's any question about the worth in your bones, or the importance of your voice, then may this serve as a reunion for you and this truth: you are worthy, abundantly so.

WHO TOLD YOU?

I do not remember the first time
I was told that my body was not good
but I do know how deeply this disembodied root goes
How much I still have to fight myself
to look in the mirror
bare-bodied naked
How I still cover in shame after intimacy
with my own husband
wondering if I am crushed petal or desired rose
I remember feeling like
I could not be one
with a body that was told it was only temptation
something to be feared and controlled
not adorned, loved, enjoyed
I still remember feeling like I had a body less desired
not one to be asked out, or kissed under bleachers or
late-night park stars,
but priding myself in such because,
ain't this the holy path?
ain't this the set-apart life?
all while I prayed in quiet for a hand
to press itself warm against my sides
I went to a nude beach once
I sat there, still a little bit hinged

◆

topless in my underwear on a beach towel

felt the sun on my full chest for the first time

walked to the shore and let the crisp ocean waves

kiss my feet and urge me to listen closely,

"I am always this way,

I am always naked as you'd say"

She whispered with every crash

tickling the sand with her salty fingers

Who told you, you were naked?

Who told you, you were naked anyway?

Who told you to hide, to play small

to dismiss your body

like it is not the greatest magic sorcery known to humankind

Just as complex as galaxies yet to be discovered?

Who told you it was anything less than wonder

that there was anything to be afraid of?

and don't you know that powerful beings

can only be stuffed down for so long

before they break the very walls that hold them,

this body

a force

wise and wild

bare-bodied glory

dips and curves

dimples and shakes

unashamed

how you gonna hide what you already are?

how you gonna live like you ain't already free?

how's it feel to break the walls

that tried to hold you?

how's the sun on your bare chest

and tell me, love,

who told you that you were naked anyway?

SHAPE-SHIFTER

when your voice begins to shift,

do not be afraid in which way it moves

do not be alarmed at the way it dives deeper

into a core you didn't know existed

do not be alarmed how it wakes up,

shakes up the depths of you

or how it allows you to find God

even still in all the mess, in all the questions

how could we ever assume that God

was not God amidst the mess,

soul deep with us, in the questions

as if my God was afraid to get her hands a little dirty

does not meet me in the wondering

what if who you are

and who you were

are competing for the whole of you?

you cannot live on a balance beam

of being two humans

you are allowed to

change and grow as time allows

you have permission to be who you want to be

in all the shapes in which you will become

may you learn to embrace the rhythm of change,

may you learn to shift with it

sometimes the shifting feels like the breaking

but, love, breathe deeply

this is the shaping

PERMISSION TO DANCE

and for once in my life
I don't want the safety net
I don't want the cool calm and collected,
calculated or controlled
I want frenzy and chaos
I want uncomfortable wild and untamed
I want to move where the wind takes me
get lost in my body
so much so it makes you wonder,
what is a body anyway?
we all need a little reckless, a little wild
hair blowing in the breeze
breath in our lungs
because it reminds us how to be alive
see everyone is a wildflower in their own time
and sometimes we just want someone to show us
that we're more than a weed.
and even when we don't admit it,
we're all waiting for someone who will tell us
that it's okay to move how we were made to
to root where we are planted

and to bloom without judgment

when we are ready to

we're all looking

for even just the slightest

permission to dance

THE WILD WITHIN

do not be afraid of your wild,

because if it were not for the untamed parts of us,

we would never really know what it means to be free

only know beauty as something to be caged

poked at and perfected

and not seamless and already part of our existence

do not be afraid of your wild

of the stallion that lives inside of you

of the parts of you that do not fit within society's perspective

    of acceptable

do not hush your wild,

do not tell her that she does not belong

because one day—while everyone scrambles to find who

    they are again—

she will bring you back to the song of your truth

to the wild in your step

and the rhythm of your heart that only your soul knows

    the beat to

she will be the one to whisper:

"keep dancing"

even when no one else hears the music

Releasing Old Stories

It's early 2022, and I'm currently in a three-week online acting intensive. It's been one of the most beautiful, disorienting, and life-giving ways to start the year. So far the scripts we've worked on have been comedy based with some real cheeky lines, where the banter is light and fast and charismatic. Having a theater background, I have always associated myself with being deep and in the moment and serious and (sometimes) overly intimate. I like connection, I love non-surface-level moments, and I love feeling things strongly and bringing others into that space through my performance. Though some of these scenes have threads of seriousness to them, their through lines are punchy and comedic.

In reflection time at the end of class, we share how we feel about the work we are doing. I keep sharing that I don't feel like a funny person (even though, truth be told, I laugh at my own corniness on the *daily*). In the last class, a coach gives me a note I'll carry with me into everything I do. She quickly chimes in and says, "I think you should stop telling that story. You say you aren't funny and comedic, but you are, you are funny. That's an old story and you should stop telling yourself that." I think back to all the stories I've told myself and keep telling myself even though they don't serve me any longer. Like how I can currently be in a fulfilling relationship and yet still be telling myself the old story that I am "a lot" or "too much" for my partner. Or the old story I would tell myself about how "humble" I was, which meant making myself small, not being honest about the gifts I know I possess, and putting myself in positions that diminish my abilities.

Simply put, old stories keep you from hearing the new ones.

The old stories about who you were and have operated as before keep you from seeing who you are and how you operate best right now, right here. Old stories keep you from seeing the fullness that God places before you every single day. Old stories keep you hearing the same song over and over again, and you may think that's just how music is, instead of listening to the new melodies that are being woven all around you. Old stories are eventually meant to be laid to rest. They don't serve where you're going or who you're becoming. And if you're not careful, those old stories will play on a loop and keep you from moving forward. Though the old story may have served you at one point, it is only holding you back now.

So if you need it, here it is: This is your reminder to stop telling the old stories. Leave room for a little awkwardness in the silence while you tune your ears to hear the new story unfolding.

THE ART OF LOVING YOURSELF
(PART 1)

learn to be okay with facing the quiet

or the chaos of your own mind,

of your own body, of your own space

Unpack the bags,

take off your shoes,

and when you find that you

no longer desire to run or to hide

when you find that you

are too much light to stay in the darkness,

open the blinds,

let the light touch your skin

marvel in it

dance with it,

let it awaken something

new in you

POWER WITHIN

There is something stirring in all of us,

a roar waiting to be released,

a strength waiting to be seen

a power nestled within the depth of each of us

a power that declares just how bold,

just how beautiful

just how capable

just how enough we truly are

not quite on the surface,

not visible enough

for everyone to see or take

or understand

but it is there,

a roar waiting to be released,

a strength waiting to be seen

a power nestled within the depth of each of us

so dig deep baby,

and listen closely

to the power within

DEEP WATERS

The ocean does not apologize

for the space that it takes up

it does not make excuses for the depths

that most people cannot handle

it cannot help but drown those who are

not ready to submerge beneath its fathomless waves

let this too be a lesson to us,

that we may expand as far as we need to

not apologize for the way others

are not ready to submerge into our waters

for those who might tell us to come back to shore

when we've always known

we were made

shaped

created

for deep waters

The Beckoning

I once cried during a podcast interview. Well, let's be honest, I've cried during a few podcast interviews, but there was one particular episode during which the host asked me about one of my poems that mentions the movie *Moana*. I get really emotional when talking about movies that I receive deep messages or confirmations from (which is a lot of them). When you break down *Moana*, the main character is constantly being told by those who don't agree with her to remember "her place" and "where she belongs." They want Moana to stay small, stay put, and stay in rhythm with what is deemed the norm of the society around her. They do this with good intentions, of course, because where Moana is experiencing fullness of identity and freedom, they are experiencing trauma and pain in their own lives. Her awareness of herself, and her listening to the beckoning toward *the more*, triggers their stronghold of fear. The fear of the "what if" and the assumption that every scenario will end up the same as before.

But in their protectiveness of her, they are also stifling the voice of the Divine (the ocean), which is calling her to *more* than the past, *more* than the pain, calling her toward the direction she has been destined and designed for. Luckily for us, as people who may also be searching for our beckoning to the more, Moana doesn't stay put. She listens to the pull, she follows the wild and unpredictable call to the ocean leading her to her purpose. And then (spoiler alert!) her freedom breaks generational strongholds of fear and the good girl conditioning. Her seemingly disobedient and defiant ways restore healing, break chains, and bring light back to her society for generations to come. She has the ability to listen to her calling, which she *knew* she was destined for, despite the noise of others' fears, despite the pull back from people she's known and loved. She knows who and where God is calling her to be and go. She knows that despite how new and unfamiliar it is, how scary and disorienting it may seem at first glance, she is being pulled into the depths of *more than she could ever ask or imagine* and past the horizons of what was initially deemed possible.

I cried when passionately sharing this revelation because I had been experiencing this same calling to be and to go. It was also scary and disorienting, but I could feel the pull beyond what was familiar or safe. Though I wasn't embarking across great oceans to restore the heart of the goddess Te Fiti, I was treading my own waters of entering into a relationship that wasn't what others may have wanted or expected of me. I was entering a space where spiritually I felt God was calling me to a deeper purpose, past what I knew or had assumed about life and love. And most important, I had to dismantle the beckoning of the voices of those around me and find the Divine distinction in the waves, the voice of my Creator, God, Love, and Light. After one of the last interventions, out of a handful from those close to me, trying to get me to not marry the love of my life, I ended the conversation with "What you're asking me to do is not go where I believe God is calling me to go next, and that's not fair." Of course that was denied, but I knew deep down that if this next, new season was a risk, it was one I was willing to take in order to become the most full, embodied, whole version of myself. I knew, outside of the boxes of comfort and

◆

familiarity, of tradition and religious tendencies, I was being called to more. My "more" in that moment was choosing my life partner despite who tried to convince me to do otherwise. My "more" in that moment was deciding to embrace a community of faith that was expansive, not afraid of the doubts or questions, and to live like Jesus in a way that challenged the doctrines I had grown up with.

I hope that you listen to the Divine calling you to more. That you don't allow fear to keep you in shallow waters, that you wade deep and wide into the expansion, whether it be yours or others', of all that you can be. I hope that you listen to the gentle beckoning of the unfamiliar as it guides you to your full, embodied, whole version of yourself and that at the other end of the risk, you find freedom. I hope the beckoning is louder than the conditioning and that you allow yourself to be pulled into the fullness of what you have been designed and destined for. So grab your sail, love (or however that process works), and whatever trusty companion(s) you need to wade through this next season, because though it may be rocky at first, it is worth it.

Yes, it is terrifying.

Yes, it will feel earth-shattering, because *it is.*

Your ability to say yes to the beckoning *is* shattering the foundations of what was to make room for the core of what will be. I believe that more terrifying, however, is if we ultimately ignore the oceans that draw us in closer, if we ignore the call to experience fullness and *choose* to stay in the small space that we are boxed into.

So, my love, let the sand guide you.

Let the ocean whisper your name.

Let it remind you that you have always, always been made

for vast depths and wide horizons.

Small was never meant to be an identity for you.

Follow the beckoning call to more.

BECKONING

sometimes fear is not always there to push you away

but instead invites you to lean in close

sometimes fear beckons you to the edge of your discomfort

and shows you the fullness of what you are made of.

sometimes fear says,

"I know it feels terrifying but come closer,

you may not be able to see it yet

but this will not break you,

only shape you"

yes sometimes fear is not about the running

but about the beckoning

into your becoming

What does Awakening look like for you right now?
What sleeping parts of you do you feel are waking up?

_____

Ask yourself these questions: Who have I been?
Who am I being? Who do I want to become?

_____

What "used to" statements about yourself came to mind
while reading this section? Who did you used to be or what
did you used to do, and how much of that has changed?

_____

What old stories do you need to stop telling yourself?

_____

What might need to change in your life, but the fear
of failure or that it won't turn out how you hope
might be stopping you?

_____

What or who does God look like to you right now
at this moment? Where do you find connectedness
with God the most?

_____

What is something that is beckoning for you and
you alone to pay attention to?

_____

The
Eclipsing

ccording to NASA, there are two types of eclipses on Earth: an eclipse of the moon and an eclipse of the sun. If you've ever witnessed an eclipse, specifically a lunar one, there is a darkness that takes over in the moment when it occurs. It seems like an infinite darkness, a never-ending shadowing, but in reality it is truly only a moment. For the sake of this book, the shadowing is the time in your life when you experience a dark space of uncertainty before the light of your own solar or lunar existence is revealed. It's a time where you can be broken open, broken down, or broken apart. I can only begin to explain the buckets of tears I cried for months on end, the sleep I could never find, the mornings I'd wake up again emotionally hungover from confusion and frustration. Months of feeling as though I had to defend what I wanted and prove that I was stepping boldly, not fearfully, into something new. Sometimes during The Eclipsing, you will notice when the shadows being cast over you are not from your own darkness but shadows that belong to others.

I had been dating John for six months when we started talking about marriage. John was the first guy I'd really ever fully dated, and when I brought him home to meet my family, it was because I already knew, from the moment I met him, that he was going to be my husband (which now, looking back at it, feels *very* bold of me to say). I wanted to bridge my different worlds, my past, present, and future all meeting and colliding in one moment. So I brought home this tatted, mystical, bright-eyed and beautiful, curious historian to meet my traditional, wonderful, Baptist parents and my protective and loving siblings. I didn't notice this until later on, but I realized what I had *really* done was not just bring home someone I was and am deeply in love with. I also was showing those who had once known me that there were parts of me that were just fully coming into the light. These parts of me could no longer be hidden because here was John, this physical representation of my awakened core, the person I was deciding to give my heart to. It wasn't that I had been purposely hiding this version of myself but my intimate conversations had happened only with close friends and questions I had brought only to trusted mentors. There was a swirling of curiosity and expansion that had happened in small bursts before I began to unfold completely.

What I thought would be a joy-filled time turned into a shadow season. One that lasted for months on end and still holds some residual tension and painful memories. In this Eclipsing space, the voices of others kept me from staying true to my own. The constant reminders of how I "should" be and who I "should" marry became the recurring narratives in my head. I couldn't trust myself or many of the people around me. I felt cynical, unbalanced, and disoriented night after night, day after day, the very threads of who I was and what I'd thought up until that moment unraveling with every passing moment.

No one really talks about the tension, uprooting, and dismantling that can come with a wedding engagement. They talk about the bliss, they show the photos of surprise and joy and confetti, but they do not show the grief that can carry itself along with your newfound love. They do not show you the upset family members because your spouse of choice is not one that they had expected and prayed for. They do not show you that in the same moment you are saying yes to one thing, you could be dismantling the structure of something else. We see the beach pictures, the laughs, the smiles and sweet kisses, but what we don't see is every conversation, every moment when that couple had to fight for the forever they wanted to say yes to, and I can't even begin to imagine what that season looks like for my LGBTQ+ loved ones. I had lived so much of my life under the applause of being the "good girl," making decisions that put others before myself, and here I was, wanting to choose the best yes I could make (in that moment), but it was met with tension. There was no doubt in my mind that John was my person, but the doubt of others started to blur my own thoughts. I had to sift through many thoughts and fears to decide which were my own and which were not.

In a solar eclipse, two shadows occur: the first is the "umbra" (UM-bruh), which leads to total eclipse, and the second is the "penumbra" (pe-NUM-bruh), or partial eclipse. By staying present in this season of engagement—not spiritually bypassing or diminishing the necessary though hard, lonely, and disorienting season—I lived through a year that felt like an umbra, a total eclipse.

The eclipse occurred in my personal life, but it also continued in 2020, with the rise of racial injustices left and right, happening to not only my own Black brothers and sisters but also brown hues of every shade, facing traumatic experiences one after another. I found myself numbed and overwhelmed at story after story about another life taken, another moment when we were reminded that justice does not ring for us. I spilled poems out of anger, out of frustration, out of sadness and fear, and tried to reconcile what it all looked like as an artist to speak life where there was so much death.

I imagine that you have experienced seasons in your life when it felt as though only this darkness surrounds you and you're not sure if there is light on the other side. Maybe you're in that season right now. Eclipsing can be hard, painful, and lonely, but it's an important step in our growth. If I've learned anything from this Unfolding process, it's that even as we sit in the darkness, we hold space for the shadows and know that beautiful things can still be birthed from them.

BECOMING

though painful at times,

do not disrupt the process

that will result in your becoming

becoming new,

becoming whole

coming back

but not as you left

do not be afraid to sit

in the beautiful tension

that growth is birthed out of

LET GO

this anxiety is not my own

this anxiety is not my own

this anxiety is not my own

I will put down what is not mine to carry

AND EVEN IN ALL THE
weariness,
I PRAY THAT
joy still
MEETS YOU.

SAY IT OUT LOUD

DE

CON

STRUC

TION

In some forms of haiku,

there is a rhythm to follow

Syllables dissecting words

breaking down the very structure

of their meanings

Almost as if it brings the very core

Of its definition into the light,

peaking in the in between

DE

CON

STRUC

TION

a word often

demonized and

dripped in condemnation

Used as a lever to pull people out of the questions

and into certainty we only think we have

the art of dismantling,

The craftsmanship of the careful eye

The heart of the vagabond

The beckoning of a call into deeper

that we can't help but listen to

The exploration of finding

the invisible bridge between

Text and meaning

discovering the richness

In the honey again

DE

CON

STRUC

TION

this is not the call of those losing their faith,

this is the process of deepening it

of expanding the notion that we have everything figured out

and instead a posture of open hands

a listening ear to the whisper of the unknown

and the mystery in the in between

Rattled

The week John and I got engaged, I had some conversations with those who expressed their concerns if John was the right partner for me. After one particularly difficult phone call, I fell to the floor weeping, yelling, begging, praying that God would show me what it was that I was supposed to do here. What was I supposed to change, surrender, or relinquish? Was it John? Or was it living up to others' expectations, even though they weren't my own? The next day, I archived our engagement photos from Instagram and took off my ring. Drama, I know, but at the time it felt so necessary.

This constant back-and-forth lasted up until John and I said, "I do." I sat up late at night, questioning my own intentions, doubting my own heart's yearning, and I ignored my own wisdom and discernment. I grew sick with anxiety and dizzy with indecisiveness about everything. I loved John with my whole heart one moment and the next it felt so very wrong to do so. I was in turmoil. There was so much noise that I couldn't hear even the sound of my own steady heartbeat, and I continuously ignored my gut knowing.

In a space where I felt I didn't know who to trust, in these dark days of my Eclipsing, I reached out to friends and mentors, people who knew me individually and also people who knew us as a couple. I like to say that these are my safety-net people and the voices that talked me off a very scary ledge. They are the people who spoke life into the future John and I were building. They saw where we were going and invited us in, embraced us, and did not bring their fears with them. These were the voices that brought me back to my own, that became the mirror in which I could seek my own reflection again. They were the lighthouses that shone through a fog, beckoning me toward the light.

They taught me that I needed to listen, not always to the voices of others, and find the balance of also listening to the still-small voice inside of me, a knowing, discerning voice, the voice of God, something that had always been there, but I had forgotten what it sounded like, until then.

LISTEN

there will be times

when the sound of your own voice feels distant

when the sound of your own thoughts feels unfamiliar

there will be times

when you are unsure if the raging inside of you is even

    your own

or something you accidentally picked up along the way

there will be times

when you must shut out the noise around you

in order to find solace in the silence inside of you

when you discover that the humming, all this time, was

    a roaring

stirring in the corners of where courage meets you in

    the mirror

the reorienting of your own voice yet again

a voice that has always been there

waiting,

for your return

GOOD FOR YOU

you know it was good for you

that the sand needed to slip through your fingers

when you look at the pile you've created,

and have no desire to pick it up

when you look behind you,

and have no desire to go back

you know you are stretching,

when the pain that comes with staying the same

hurts worse than the pain it takes to grow

good for you, love,

this is growing

IN SYNC

everyone experiences hard moments in life

the moments that make, break, and shape you

the experiences that pull who you truly are from your core

and challenge it to stare at your present reflection

the reflection you can't run from

because it's who you are

and if you stare hard enough,

you will find hope

you will find beauty

you will find the one thing that makes

staring at all that you are

seem less daunting, less terrifying

you will find someone else

staring at their reflection too

and it won't feel so lonely anymore

you won't feel so crazy anymore

time will stop for a moment,

let you gasp for air

and remind you that you are alive

right now

breathing

barely, but breathing

and there is someone, something

an entity bigger

than you can know or fathom,

always by your side

breathing steadily, gently

along with you every step of the way

WEARY HEARTED

for the weary hearts and tender souls,

for the sensitive spirits and exhausted bodies,

tread gently with your humanity,

for it is the only one you'll ever have

listen to the ache and whispers of your being

be kind, let go, release what keeps you from seeing the
    sunshine in your very veins

for the world around you may get heavy, so by all means rest
    until you rise again

for there is a dawn, every time you exhale and a glorious rise
    within every breath

See Me

In 2016, after yet another viral video of race-related violence, this time of Philando Castile, was everywhere, I wrote my poem "Human." It was the first poem I ever wrote about police violence and brutality, the first poem in which I grappled with the weight of being Black in America. Growing up Christian, I had been taught my identity had to do with our Evangelical faith and not necessarily our race. We grew up knowing that we were children of God, that we were blessed and highly favored (amen), but not necessarily that we were *Black*, blessed, and highly favored (amen again). Though I am grateful for this shaping, I also now see the things I did not know or see, or was initially sheltered from, in regards to being so Black, blessed, and highly favored.

"Human" broke me open in so many ways, as it was the first time I had really put to paper how angry, hurt, and scared I was. It made me realize how unsafe I truly felt, even in environments where I thought I was embraced and accepted for *all* of me (including my Blackness). From the nights when I was a freshman in college, where I tucked under my covers as deep as possible so that my roommates couldn't see me put on my head wrap for my hair at night, only to hear them whispering in "concerned" voices about why they couldn't see my hair, and if I was wrapping it because I had a disease that caused hair loss. To being told that I was only given opportunities to speak on stage because I was an "acceptable" type of Black person. To realizing that in church spaces I craved more than just sprinkles of color in the seats around me. "Human" made me wrestle with the reality that with my privilege, my only "I'm a Christian in

America" lens, had caused a blindness to so much happening around me. In that poem, I came to terms with my fear about my big and tall father and brother, who could be seen as threats simply for being. I came to terms with the fears I had about what weight I would carry if I too were to marry a Black man and how much I would fear for his life daily.

It has been almost six years since I wrote that poem, and those words, those fears, those wrestlings, are still very present realities for so many Black and brown people in our society. The death of Breonna Taylor felt like the death of a sister to me. There was a movement going around at the time of Breonna's birthday in June 2020 in which artists and all who were willing were challenged to send a birthday card in honor of Breonna to the city officials in order to bring forth accountability for her death. I stood in the birthday card aisle of Rite Aid, stumped as to what kind of card you are supposed to get for a stranger who will never even be able to see it. I found myself drawn to the "Sister" section of cards and settled on one. It felt so fitting because, from the photos to the video clips, I wept for her the way I would have wept for a sister.

The weekend after our wedding, while I was still sitting in my own shadows of personal Eclipsing that accompanied the tension our marriage brought, there was a vigil being held for George Floyd and a community of people flooded a courtyard and the streets of Pasadena to hold silent for eight minutes and forty-six seconds, the amount of time it was first reported he was held, to his death, against his will. I stood there, with my new husband, along with friends of all races and ethnicities, and tears slowly began to trickle down scattered faces as we held the tension and the silence but for a moment this solidarity was healing.

In between all this grieving were waves of watered-down social media justice calls, initiatives to "pass the mic" and "follow a fellow Black person," some of which were beneficial, but most were short-lived, performative, and transactional. In those waves, my social media following grew by the thousands. At first, it was exciting to finally be recognized as a creator and artist worth following, but the excitement soon diminished into an overwhelming fog and I felt as though people were only there to watch my Blackness or my grief or my anger. While I was trying to hold, process, and not internalize the pain and the grief, I was given a weird platform to be a spokesperson for something I know only from experience and not expertise. I (sometimes) know how to be human, I know how to be the best Black Woman version of myself I can be, I know how to share traditions related to me and my family, and I know how to string together pain in metaphors (sometimes), but I do not always know how to guide people in understanding what all of that is like.

My goal as an artist, as a communicator, as a wordsmith, is to be a bridge. To understand that there is always a thread that connects us to each other whether we see it or not. A bridge to connect the space between "us" and "them," between "here" and "now," between my humanity and yours, and to remember that the distance between is so much shorter than we have been led to believe.

◆

HUMAN

I should not have watched the video
I should not have clicked the hashtag trail that led me
    to your tombstone
I should have grieved you as distant Black woman
but I cannot stay as distant Black woman
when anger and hurt and fear all make parading music
    in this chest
I did not have the sound on
I did not want to hear your pleas or their yelling false lies
    into your identity
I only saw white holding on to black bear
while still trying to prove that though big, not a threat
my body heaved forward when I saw the way the bullet
    undid your thirty-seven years of life
took dignity, took breath
took father from son
and husband from wife
you are the one hundredth, no, the five hundredth . . .
the numbers have gone rapid and without proper watch
because they are spiraling out of control
we have not spiraled out of control
we have not burned down bridges,
we have tried instead to cross them

we have not threatened lives we are just trying to save

our own

when was it that you took us for threats?

Took us as a war on your country so much that you must

genocide Black people?

when did our melanin become the picture for your insecurity?

did our educated tongues and demands to be human make

your supremacy flinch?

My father though big not a threat

my mother Black skin, Black woman, Black strong

my brother lean and tall and Black

my sisters, beautiful

magic and Black

they are my blood

they are this blood

that at any time could be massacred on sidewalks filmed

with phones

this is the only way to mark this history

this is the only way to prove we still exist

we are still here

we are still pleading

tired but pleading

and it terrifies me to love a Black man because is that not the

same as strapping a ticking time bomb to your heart and

waiting for the timer to go off?

Is it not the same as holding on to something that the world
    says you cannot have?
It feels like a premade noose around my family tree I have yet
    to add my own branches to
is it not the same as giving birth to ashes?
because I fear my children will never know what life looks
    like without death always taunting on our doorstep
I was made Black
I was born Black and I am Black
I am loud voice because instead of lungs God gave me a
    megaphone
and he nudged me after so many times
after so many deaths
after so many names
God tugged me,
said *when are you going to use this voice that I have given you to*
    shake people into feeling
shake the separation from our tongues and do your best to bring
    unity back into these hands?
a few weeks ago my family and I went to a restaurant,
grabbed hands, bowed our heads,
and closed our eyes to pray, and I wondered,
what if we don't open them again?
Because someone decides that we are not as human as them
that we are threats, that we are mass destructions posed as
    humbled heads

how much more will we weep?

How many lives will have hashtags for tombstones?

Do we need to scream louder?

We are human. We are human. We are human.

We are alive. We are real. **We are human.**

Perhaps this will all cease and we will know peace

when there are enough tears shed that we all start drowning

I do not know if you pray

I do not know how you pray

but if this does not bring us to bended knees then I don't

　　know what mercy was made for

and lately

my prayers have looked a lot like,

Jesus if you come back, can you just say one thing?

"I made them too, I created them too"

we are not taking up any more space than we have

　　intended to

our bodies do not spell out war

we just want to know that we can fall asleep

wake up the next day

and not wonder

if our Black will look like less

less human

we want to sit down at our dinner tables

and not have to mourn over another lost brother or sister

when you sit at your dinner table

do you mourn over another lost brother or sister

God made us too,

we are not taking up any more space than we were made to

our bodies do not spell out war

So please

hands up

don't shoot

LET US BREATHE

and we run too fast so they stop us

we glow too bright so they become our shadows

we're too beautiful,

and unfamiliar to their normality,

so they call us dangerous

we can't just be great,

we must be perfect

and you wonder why we protest

and you wonder why we make safety,

make beauty,

make movements only for us

let Black women be great

in fact, just let Black women be

SAY HER NAME

where is her protest?

where is the rage burning for the female body?

not televised, not recorded

her death, not a silent act

a violent exchange of bullet to skin

eight times

her screams, her cries

still echoing off the walls of an apartment

once home, now a battleground

she was a brief moment,

a hashtag

her life a brief moment

the fury diminished to fumes

her murderers home,

sitting comfortably

her body home,

sitting restless underground

do not forget about the Black woman

do not forget about the chest that kept you

or the hands that held you

they say seven is the number of completion

so the irony of you not experiencing your twenty-seventh

    birthday

sits as acidic as the blood seeped into your apartment carpets

we are a year apart

twenty-seven was the year I found myself

was the year I found how to speak the name God on my

   tongue again,

the year I found love

the year I lived life to the fullest

your life . . . cut short,

unplugged

wiped from the story

I pray you lived your best year

I pray you found yourself before you lost her

I pray that as the bullets hit you, God held you in the

   same breath,

while you breathed your last breath

I am sorry your life could not have seen fullness,

could not have reached completion

your body may be buried, love,

but your name will not be

Breonna Taylor

Suffering

IS OFTEN THE ENTRYWAY FOR BREAKTHROUGH AND BECOMING. IT CAN BE PAINFUL, AND OFTEN IT FEELS LIKE A **DEATH** BECAUSE SOMETIMES THAT'S EXACTLY WHAT IT IS. The old is dying; THE NEW IS being birthed.

NIGHTMARE

do the tears ever stop?

do the brown bodies ever live?

we are past tired, past angry

the overflow of emotions that

our ancestors were not given space to feel

we are numb

from feeling the same

thing over and over again

we are numb from seeing the same thing

over and over again

if I just wake up,

maybe this nightmare will be over

BLACK BREATH

And with a collective exhale
all the Black Bodies sighed
we have been holding our breath
for longer than we can count now
our fists, still raised
but for a moment they rest,
wrapped over one another
in a sigh of relief
justice, for once,
has been served—
whatever that even means anymore
we have so much more work to do
but for this moment, we can breathe
we breathe for all the bodies who cannot
we breathe,
we love,
we fight for those taken
we have so much more work to do
but for this moment,
we inhale hope
and we breathe

LADY FREEDOM

I had a dream that I met freedom. She sat there with a cigarette clenched in between calloused and wrinkled hands. She looked at me with tired eyes and sighed,

"Do not believe the lie. Don't let them convince you into believing that you have to earn me, find me, or chase me."

She said out of the corner of lazy lips wrapped around paper with tiny fireworks on the end,

"Don't let them trick you into believing it's not already yours. No need to find me, no need to earn me, pointless to chase. Instead stand there, still. Head raised high. Show them you cannot and will not chase what is already yours."

She drew one last inhale and I saw where the stars used to be in her eyes.

HOLD THE DOOR

Life is so strange sometimes,

it does not stop

not for death,

not for moments of rest

not for moments to exhale

It is up to each of us to lean into the pauses,

it's up to each of us to choose to hold for the confetti toss,

to listen to the hearts that stop

and the tears that fall

we must hold space

for it all

because life will not

hold the door for anyone

or anything

it will just

keep

going

HUMAN(KIND)

In a society that thrives on individualism,
we sometimes forget the gift that is each other
we forget how beautiful our hearts sound
when they are in sync with one another
this humanity
the greatest symphony
the orchestras that our whole beings long for
who are we to be without touch,
without the laughter that swells from
the deepest joys and the greatest sorrows
without empathy that swells
from the core of our one heartbeat
so let's call this the comeback,
the remix that we keep missing.
the part two
the music of you
and the music of me
and ain't it beautiful

A FLOWER

NEVER HAS TO ASK FOR PERMISSION
TO GROW OR BLOOM.
IT DOES SO BECAUSE IT
WAS MADE TO, AND, MY LOVE,
so are you.

THE ART OF FEELING

You beautiful feeling being
full of heart and soul
carrying grief and joy
sometimes in the same breath
attempting to find rhythms that keep you grounded
anthems of *"Be where your feet are"*
when the ground beneath you is steadily shifting
this year has not been the most gentle
or the most kind
but it has been the most shaping and chiseling
calling the human being
out of your existence and hushing the doing
causing you to still
to heal
to feel
everything
but look at how far you've come,
look at how beautifully you've arrived,
you have made it so far,
to the bliss of winter, the music of a turning page
this chapter, beginning to close,
though there is no wrapping of bows in this final moment
look at the story that has unfolded
one of grief and sadness

◆

one of hope and loss

one of insurmountable joy and stunning surprises tucked in

do not hold back,

do not suppress

shed every tear

laugh with all the joy that sorrow could not take from you

carry all the joy you can grasp in your palms

find familiarity in the twinkle of lights,

as they light up your eyes

the smell of home bringing you back,

this is where your feet are

this is where you find your breath again

find your breath again

and feel all the feelings

every single one of them

you glorious feeling being full of life

full of life

HOPE

Hope has come lately in varying forms
in little victories, in sunsets and sunrises
and the glisten in his eyes
Hope has shown
its face to us in many ways,
in the breath we breathe every day
in the breeze of the wind,
being the closest form of a hug for most of us
reminding us of how much
we can finally release
a change of pace,
a needle of hope underneath
the debris of so much loss
so much grief
hope holds our faces close
in the cup of its hands
gently kisses our tears
and whispers,
even the darkness at some point ends

KNOW THAT YOU CAN HOLD ALL THE GRIEF,
ALL THE SADNESS AND CONFUSION,
AND IT WILL NOT MAKE A
home out of you.
YOU WILL COCOON WITH UNCERTAINTY
BUT EMERGE WITH WINGS OUTSTRETCHED,
glowing AND renewed.

Letting Go

So there's going to be some loss, there's going to be shedding, there's going to be grief that might feel unfathomable, unfixable, or untolerable. It might feel like the walls are closing in, that you're losing yourself in the madness of it, but here's the beautiful part of it: as you sift through those ashes, you find what's coming, you find a small bud somehow sprouting through the concrete, covered in dust, inviting you to brush it off. Blow on it gently and watch this new thing evolve and become. And maybe, when the lights turn on or after you've learned how to adjust your eyes to the momentary darkness, you'll find that all along you are that bud waiting to bloom.

Reflect on a season of your life that felt like an Eclipsing season. What brought you there? What did it feel like in the midst of it? If you're experiencing an Eclipsing right now, describe what it feels like at this very moment. (Before writing, take a breath and know that this season will pass. Know that you have made it through so much, and even if you have further to go, you have so much to be proud of.)

What lessons have your Eclipsing seasons taught you? What qualities have they brought out in you?

What tools and resources helped you see the light, as you started to emerge from your Eclipsing? If you're in the midst of this Eclipsing, what resource or tool do you think would help you in this moment?

Think of a time when hope has shown up for you in your life. Was it a kind word from a stranger, a thoughtful gesture by a friend, an inspiring quote you came across, or something else?

_____

Write a letter to yourself for the next Eclipsing season that comes your way. Write words of encouragement that would help you to navigate that season.

_____

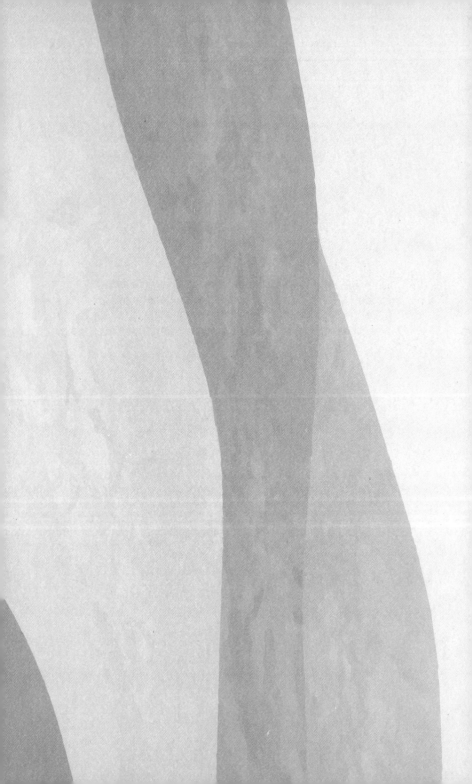

The Mending

intsugi is the Japanese art form of repairing broken pottery pieces with lacquer that includes powdered gold, silver, or platinum. *Kintsugi* can take many forms and has connections to a handful of philosophical ideas, like the philosophy of *wabi-sabi*, which is the seeing of beauty in the flawed or imperfect. The method is also connected to the feeling that the Japanese refer to as *mottainai*, an expression of regret when something is wasted, with a connection to *mushin*, which is the acceptance of change. This art form reminds us that even those things that seem broken or unrepairable can still become something beautiful. Also, that we don't have to be pretty or pristine in order to be considered whole or worthy.

When we walk through The Eclipsing, we are surrounded by the broken pieces of what was once our life and our identity. The Mending allows us to bring those pieces back together.

Some pieces are worth keeping, not to be wasted, and some we must grieve and release because they no longer serve where we're going. Like the art of *kintsugi*, we can bring those pieces together into something new and beautiful.

For me, what The Mending process looked like was first healing my relationship to God and spirituality. In The Awakening and The Eclipsing seasons, I became aware that I had associated the voice of God with the voice of those closest to me. In this Mending space, I had to release those voices and welcome in and restore the voice of God. Was God loving? Or judging? Was God speaking guilt or shame over me, or was God's intention to take those things away from my identity and restore the truth of who I am? Does God dictate or does God guide in love? I will not tell you that I have nailed this process quite yet, because to be honest, most days I still feel as though I am in the thick of that unlearning, but I do have a better grasp on that voice, that beckoning. Yes, God speaks to me in love, yes, God seeks to take the shame off me, yes, God speaks infinitely into the truth of who I am, loved, capable, and seen.

In that same space of Mending and reclaiming the voice of God in my soul, there was also the reclaiming of my body. I had spent almost thirty years believing that what mattered most was my spirit, my soul, which I still believe to be true, but I learned that it doesn't end there. I was taught to ignore the flesh because it'll get you into trouble, but in the Unfolding, I realized that my flesh, my body, gave me more guidance than she was given credit for. For so long I didn't know how to live in my physical body because I had been told to make it less than. I gradually realized that this body is the only home I'll ever know, so why would I not learn all the beautiful, intimate, and glorious ways to be here? I started to show more of this exploration in my creativity and my photographs, posing in two-piece swimsuits (Oh my) and dancing in my underwear. I had to come to a point where I mended both body and soul, heart and mind, back in union with one another so that I knew how to be intimate, aware, and in tune not only in my relationship but more importantly with myself.

Along the same lines as ignoring or denying the importance of our physical bodies, I learned we as a society bypass grief and heartache, choosing instead to skip over those feelings with platitudes. Christians especially have a tendency to be so quick at the "God is good" comeback while masking pain and discrediting joy. Having to navigate a season of holding both grief *and* joy made me lean into both. Lean into how God could be all good and I could still be hurting equally inside. Into how I could celebrate my wedding day and also grieve the death of my uncle in the same breath. Into how I could dance and celebrate the new union of my marriage with a Zoom DJ and also sit with the weight of my community as we grieved another Black brother or sister, lost to a system that was never made to keep us safe. We are met daily with the tension of holding both grief and joy, mending the sticky tissue of the unknown with some inkling of hope that tomorrow the sun will shine on us again.

And with all of this Mending, even with the changes and shifts we are making, just when we think we've reached "the other side" and the work is done, we have moments when we backtrack into old habits and personalities for the comfort of other people who knew us as such. The Mending process,

◆

though beautiful, can also be painful because it may involve us leaving spaces, relationships, and systems that only served who we were and not who we are becoming.

The Mending process is a tender one, one that involves quiet and kind work with ourselves throughout it. When we mend something, it is with the constant reminder that healing is not a destination to reach but a constant journey, and sometimes it involves picking up the pieces alone and repairing them on our own, without the approval or applause of others. And that is okay. Because we aren't actually alone at all. We are divinely guided and infinitely held.

AUDIENCE OF ONE

so perhaps then the true test of becoming,

is the question of,

can I still become and unfold into who I am meant to be next

without the approval or applause of others

there to cheer me out of my cocoon?

what if no one is there to witness this steady and sweet

    shifting

what if the arrival for right now,

is silent like dawn

and the warmth of dew

glistening on my slowly unfolding petals

perhaps when we arrive,

no one is there to watch it unfold,

or to applaud, but we know it's happened

we know what beauty we've become

and what ashes we rose from to get there

and that then

is all that matters

for our eyes only

BEATITUDES

As I left a friend's house,

walking to my car,

she called after me,

"Be kind to yourself"

when I left my chiropractor appointment,

the doctor told me to take it easy

the wind at the park near my house

reminds me to take gentle, slow breaths

the people and places around me

have a way of tucking

the love letters I often ignore,

into my interactions with them

they remind me to move slower,

to let my body tell me when it needs to rest,

to let my mind speak kinder thoughts than I usually allow

last night,

my friend saw my phone background,

It read: *"Be kind to yourself, my love"*

and she told me to put my name in it,

to replace "love" with my own personal beckoning

be kind to yourself, <u>Arielle</u>

be kind to yourself, <u>Arielle</u>

be kind to yourself, _____

why is it less of a question

when you give kindness to someone else?

it is easy to generalize the need for

self-care and self-love for the masses

when it is your job to encourage,

to inspire, and to be the soft speaking voice of kindness

but it is much harder,

to put your name in the love notes

that you so easily give to everyone else around you

all while you remain your own worst enemy

I am learning to be less of my own worst enemy

a little softer

and a little more kind

I hope you are kind to you too

be gentle with others,

be gentle with (you)

be understanding

be grace filled

be loving

be kind

HEALERS

We get to choose

what takes our peace and what fills it.

we have the ability to press pause on chaos and

find the grounding of our own two feet again

we cannot be the healers

unless we are willing first to heal

TEND TO YOUR WOUNDS
BEFORE YOU TRY TO HEAL THE WORLD.
CRACKED VESSELS
CAN'T *hold water*;
THEY CAN ONLY RELEASE IT.

UNDONE

Transformation is not always loud,

sometimes it approaches quietly

beckons you to return to where you once were

reflecting every step on the way back

that you are not the same as when you first left

Sometimes transformation quietly

erupts inside of you,

sometimes it unfolds like lava,

slow and thick

from the inside out

sometimes change doesn't always appear

visible to the human eye

it can be subtle

a slow unraveling of a blossom

at the first sign of sunshine

the hint of moisture from the morning dew

on the edge of a new leaf

it is when you notice the change,

the transformation, that the processing begins

the realization of *oh my,*

I am not who I once was

Something has changed me

I am undone in the best way

rejoicing begins,

and declaration takes shape

on our tongues

I am not who I once was

Something has changed me

I am undone

God Moment

In January of 2020, I said yes to the opportunity to go to Israel. I said yes for various reasons: to explore the history behind the book and stories I was raised on, to travel somewhere new and share the experience with my social media community, and, lastly, to prove to myself and the questioning people in my life that I was still a "Christian."

As I mentioned in "The Awakening," this was a period of exploration, when I gave myself more permission to ask questions that I'd never asked before. I grappled with what it meant to read and understand the Bible. In the past, I'd seen the text of the Bible used as a weapon, as particular passages were used online to create separation instead of unity, to inflict pain and not healing. And then there was the way I had been raised to celebrate certainty and downplay doubt. When the Bible is seen as the ultimate truth, many times this means there's no room to poke holes or question what's in its pages, to wrestle with the context and meaning of the rich parables and the guidance given to us in the ancient text.

As I questioned the rigidity with which I had been taught to read and interpret the Bible, I also tried to remove the rigid certainty of my faith that rejected everything and everyone that wasn't considered "Christian enough." I wanted wonder, mystery, and wandering that brings you back home no matter how far and wide you may adventure. I wanted a faith that didn't leave out certain people based on their background or sexuality, as if they were any less beloved or worthy. I wanted to have "God moments" in the mundane and unassuming, in open mics and downtown bars, on porches or in passing moments, on yoga mats or during retreats in the desert.

So I went to Israel, to have an awesome "God moment" that would prove that my faith was still as vibrant as it always had been. I wanted to go to the places where scholars say Jesus walked. I wanted to expand the horizons of how I saw Jesus and his life and death and see just how much I was a part of the story too, or find if I was at all. The experience was powerful, life changing and transformative, but not in the way I had expected. Instead of experiencing it through the same strict and filtered view I had had for so long, in which everything was literal and there was no room for curiosity or space for nuances, I saw every place and every moment as raw, messy, yet still divine, and I found myself in the middle of all of it. As we walked where it is said that Jesus walked, as we sat where he could have preached and sailed on the Sea of Galilee, I kept whispering, waiting, asking for that "God moment."

When we got to the end of our trip, we checked into our last hotel. Looking around the hotel, there weren't any obvious holy tracings there, or biblical stories coming to life; instead, just a really nice, bougie hotel on the water. I placed my luggage on my bed and instantly felt a rushing need to go outside, and so I did. Just a few steps away from the hotel, I found a pathway leading to a tiny lighthouse. I took my time as I paced the pathway back and forth, knowing I was meant to stay present there for a moment. I stood facing the crashing waves as they repeatedly swept against the giant boulders beneath me, the only things keeping me from floating away into the ocean's depths.

As wave after wave crashed against the rocks and droplets of water began to cover my face, it was hard to differentiate between the salt of the sea's wet hugs and my own tears. I slowly found myself weeping, fully immersed in that moment. Salt meshing with salt, becoming one body, mind, spirit, *being*, with whatever holiness resided in the ocean. I found myself finally having the answer to all of the "Where is my God moment?" questions I had been asking for days.

I found myself almost scoffing at the sky.

"Here? In all places *this* is my *God moment*?"

"Exactly," I heard back, soft and sure.

The ocean has always been a place where I go to find calm. It's where I go to hear my own thoughts or nothing at all, the place where I can allow my heartbeat and the waves to make music in sync with each other and remind me how alive I am.

I had been afraid of losing my faith, of being disconnected from God, because I was being told that the decisions I was making were leading me down that path. But that day at the ocean in Israel started to heal something in me, remind me of something I had always known, that I hadn't lost my faith; I had just lost the pieces that no longer served where I felt God was calling me to go, into the unknown. And not necessarily the scary "Don't go, it's dark out there!" type of unknown but a childlike wonder, the "Dive into the depths of divinity" kind of unknown, to find God in all of it. I didn't *have* to travel to the other side of the world and have waves of a land I've never known call out to me and remind me that I am not far, that I have not lost sight of God and she has not lost sight of me . . . but I'm so glad I did.

◆

I know that just like life, faith is not linear. That God has never been afraid of our questions or our curious hole poking. I don't know exactly where the tomb of Jesus is or where in the desert he wandered, but I know that his death and resurrection happened for a reason, not to remind us how awful we are but to remind us how *loved* we are. I know that sometimes it still makes me cry to read scripture, but I no longer depend on the Bible as the only way God speaks. If all those ancient texts are God speaking, then who's to say that they've ever stopped?

I am not certain or sure all the time; my steps are wobbly and unpredictable, just like a balancing posture in yoga or a baby's first steps. We're all waiting for our own waves to come crashing over the rocks, waiting for God to sprinkle a little life over us, causing us to rise more boldly than before and declare, "Yes, this here is my God moment, and what a glorious moment it is."

WAVES

I am standing in the presence

of waves that crash so strongly

where I can taste and feel the salt water

splash on my face

it has been quite some time since

I have been overwhelmed with the immenseness of nature

reminding me of the immenseness of its Creator

I am standing in the presence

of salt water that wants to dance with the tears

falling down my face

and my hands can only do one thing

outstretch to receive,

to take in, to be overcome

this voice can only do one thing

worship

exalt

the glory before me

and the hands that made it all,

made me

salt and water

flesh and bones

finding our own waves and our own shores

however they come

this is the holiest of places

both wave and whisper

This, my Beloved, this is for you

SOMETIMES I JUST THINK IF WE HEARD "I'm so proud OF WHO YOU'RE BECOMING" IT WOULD BE A LESS ROCKY LANDING. WHETHER YOU HEAR THE WORDS OR NOT, I HOPE YOU HAVE THE courage TO GROUND YOURSELF ANYWAY, DESPITE HOW ROCKY THE LANDING MIGHT BE.

REPOTTING

when a plant outgrows its surroundings

it does not shrink to remain,

instead it expands

and so must its surroundings

all that to say,

you are not too much

everywhere around you is simply too small

THE ART OF LOVING YOURSELF (PART 2)

Stand up for you, stand up for all you've fought to become

do not make excuses, no more unnecessary apologies,

stop biting your tongue

when they try to convince you to go backward,

remind them that you are no longer going that way

NOTHING TO PROVE

They ask me why I pose in my underwear on social media,
ask me what it is I am trying so hard to prove.
I say, *Ain't that the reason for freedom anyway?*
that we don't have to prove anything at all
so we dance in cropped cotton bras and high-waisted
    underwear,
we pose in lace that makes us feel like whatever woman we
    want to be
without the hiding,
we reveal what has always been underneath our coverings
as they tell us to stay covered,
keep quiet, spine not so tall,
trapping us into exhaustion from holding up everyone else's
    fear of our bodies
that we no longer have for ourselves
he tells me,
only prostitutes of biblical times used their bodies
to lure people away from God
I tell him,
I am not trying to lure anyone anywhere,
I am simply trying to keep God in

There You Are

I told my therapist in a session recently that I thought I felt sad but I wasn't entirely sure why.

We sifted through the possibilities, finding that it was a toxic cocktail of anxiety, a spiral of fear of change and identity shifting. The weight of disappointing others simply by living my life. The unsettling of a world around us that felt chaotic and yet everyone operated as if we were all "fine." I left the session, not ready to relinquish the sadness yet comforted in knowing its desire to teach me.

"Find what helps you cope," she told me as I left.

And so I did what I knew best. I wrote. I spilled words and prose on a page, my mind dancing in the practical and creative. I cried, I danced, I sang, I drank wine, and then I found myself in the middle, in the mess of the process, noticing a slow return as the sadness shifted. *Oh, there I am*, I said to myself.

Sometimes our greatest tool for pulling ourselves out of the holes where we find ourselves buried is the reminder that we have access to healing. In that moment of uncertainty and sadness, I found I had everything I needed right there in my own hands, right here in my heart.

And so do you.

Peace

I want to walk you through a meditation that has helped me
find healing during my season of The Mending.
If they serve you in this moment, repeat these statements
and declare them over yourself:

I declare peace over this body.
I declare peace over my mind.

Again, but this time, if you feel safe enough to do so,
place a hand on your heart:

I declare peace over this body.
I declare peace over my mind.

And now place a palm on your forehead and press gently:

I declare peace over this body.
I declare peace over my mind.

Inhale.
Exhale.

Close all the open tabs in your mind,
calm the frenzy in your heart,
and take a deep breath—
in through your nose,
out through your nose.
Wave the white flag to the havoc inside of you.
Continue your deep breaths for as long as you need,
and return to this meditation whenever you need a reminder
that you have the peace you need, nestled within you.

LINES AND SHAPES

Shapes and lines
this body, a road map
a treasure hunt,
like galaxy shapes
and Milky Way paths
I always assumed,
that what it was leading to
was outside of me
but then I hear,
*"When you're done
with all your travel . . ."*
she whispers gently
*"Wandering to and fro
for the value of your home,
searching for safety in others,
seeking validation in mirrors,
I hope you find your way back to me"*
All these lines and shapes
ebbs and flows
have been pointing
me right back to her

◆

124

time and time again

Ah,

I exhale,

so this is the home I've been searching for

this is the home that I already am

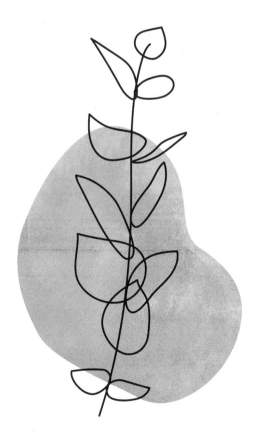

ARCHITECT

if you were a sunflower,

your stem would only know how to stand tall

facing and turning toward only the light

and not the sway of others

so, love, stand tall and face the light

stand tall even when being pushed forward

slip notes to your rising self to keep going,

so that waking up has purpose

remember that you are bursting at the seams with fighter

you are warrior overflow

these moments are stepping stones of victory to remind you

of how far you've come, of how far you will go

remind you of every brick you've laid with your own two

    hands

keep building, my love,

something beautiful, strong, and on purpose will be birthed

    from all this

Grief and Celebration

"Can we still celebrate here?" That's what I kept asking myself the week of what we had hoped would be a big and beautiful wedding to mark the rest of my life with John. Instead, the pandemic, which at this point we had been experiencing for months, was changing all those plans. "Can we still celebrate here?" I asked as, days before I was scheduled to say "I do," I stood in a hospital room, looking at my uncle—who was only breathing because of the tubes connected to him—tears streaming down my cheeks, pressing into the fabric of my mask. "Can we still celebrate here?" I asked John the night before our wedding as we looked up locations of parks near the hospital, so my mother could attend and then quickly go back to her brother's side. "Can we still celebrate here?" I asked again, witnessing injustice after injustice against Black and brown people erupting in our daily news. "Can we still celebrate here?" I asked this question almost every day in 2020, and no matter how dark and heavy the surrounding circumstances may be, the answer I have always found is yes, there is room for both celebration and grief.

When someday our kids read about this time in their history books, about lockdowns and pandemics and non-traditional weddings, when they ask John and me how we lived and how we responded to the chaos around us, we will tell them we celebrated our wedding on a Saturday where a park met a beach and overlooked horizons we couldn't even see and then we grieved the death of their great-uncle on Sunday.

We will tell them that not long after, we continued to grieve and mourn the loss of Ahmaud Arbery, Breonna Taylor, George Floyd, and those we may not even know the names of. We prayed, we lamented, we let our anger exist righteously, and we loved, deeper than before and more intimately. We danced with our friends and wedding guests whom we couldn't see in person, over Zoom, with a disco ball hanging in our tiny living room, the DJ luring us into sweat, laughter, and joy for a moment. And then the next day we mourned and prayed all over again with our community, held up tired hands and lit candles and grieved as a community just as diligently as we had celebrated.

When they ask us, I want to tell our kids that we did both, that we held both, and that there is room for both. That sometimes life will hand you grief and celebration in one breath and remind you that both can exist and can be felt fully. That there doesn't have to be one or the other but that in any given moment they both can serve as necessary and press us deeper into what it means to be human.

SAND

Sometimes life

dares you to hold the smallest pieces of grief and joy

while it slips through your fingers

like sand

and sometimes it leaves seashells in your palms

urging you to gaze at the glory of something

so fully intact after all that it's been through—

sand, water, wave, and storm.

Sometimes life

dares you to hold both joy and grief at the same time

because the sand will continue to slip

and life will continue to happen

and joy and grief will both be there

sometimes in the same breath

daring you to inhale one

while you exhale the other

and find the courage to keep on living

RISING

Have you ever watched the way a woman rises?
the way her knees first press into the ground
because she knows what it means to fall
and then to rise
have you ever watched the way a woman loves?
how she uses her hands first and then her heart second
as if she catches everyone who's ever fallen
in her steady and consistent palms
have you ever watched the way a woman dances?
how she twirls and twirls
resembling a tornado
captivating and simultaneously terrifying
a woman is a force to be reckoned with
she is not weak, she is not vulnerable
She is whirlwind of beauty
twirling and powerful,
twirling and magical.
a woman is a force to be reckoned with
not a body to be messed with
a woman is a sacred type of resilience
she is music every time she rises
she is grace every time she loves
she is freedom every time she dances

all things curve and hip, strength and safety,

both the lighthouse and the wave

both the tornado and the calm

the tide necessary for a fresh start

see, they keep searching for answers,

wondering and looking for a change

and they do not stop to think that maybe it is us

Us dancing, our exterior armor both durable and tender

both necessary in a world that keeps making us fight for
ourselves

and learning that our greatest weapon is knowing exactly who
we are

See, I refuse to be a woman

who stays unaware of the depth of my voice

and the weight of my steps.

Arielle means "lioness of God"

as if there was a roaring strength placed inside me

before I ever knew a single word

and there is a lioness in all of us

caged within our rib cages

where our breath meets our soul

she is the reminder that we all have lion-like hearts

the reminder that though we are women

who sometimes may fall,

we are also women

◆

who know what it means to rise

to fall and to rise

to fall and to rise

a reminder that even though she is down

she will, she will, get back up

What areas need Mending in your life?

Where are you noticing *kintsugi* happening either
in you or around you?

Acknowledge a place where hurt is still present
in your life. What steps can you take to move
toward healing that place?

Like the ocean for me, what places, activities,
or physical representations bring you back
to yourself?

How have you been able to hold room for both
grief and joy in your life? Is there a time or an event
that would help you to reflect back on from
this perspective?

The Illuminating

ou have journeyed now from Awakening to the shifts in your life to exposing shadow seasons to doing the work of Mending thereafter. Now, you find the space to dance and bask in the beautiful work you've done to bring out the truths of who you are. Illuminating is the phase of "letting the light in." The Illuminating space also allows you to see your blind spots and the places where you can still learn to grow and let go.

Even with all the change you've undergone, there will still be some moments when you retreat into your old roles. The Illuminating is a beautiful space where you can bask in the freedom of finding home and accepting yourself in who you are in this present moment.

For me this season became a time when I had to relinquish the idea that choosing my happiness, choosing what was best for me, was selfish. I had to be confident in the deepest part of my being that choosing the love of my whole life was worth it, even if it meant saying no to other people, to spaces I once belonged in, or dismantling other people's perceptions of me. I had to be confident that even if I pulled the thread of whimsy and wonder, I would still have faith in something bigger than me and a relationship with an all-creative, all-beautiful God. In this season there were still tears, but they were tears of release, tears of declaring, "I don't have to hold on to this anxiety, fear, sadness, grief anymore. I can make room for joy here too." In The Illuminating space there was more clarity. I wasn't saying, "I don't know," when deep down I truly did; I was speaking my truth as boldly as I could even if my voice shook.

Now that the darkness of The Eclipsing phase has passed, The Illuminating is also a space of revealing new perspectives, fresh eyes, and a new light. It is that moment when the morning comes and, as you open the blinds or curtains, the light peeks through just a little, dances on your skin, and reminds you: *Your head is above water. Breathe. Feel the light on your face again. You're okay.* You might find yourself dancing in this season or you might find yourself weeping at all the loss and release you just experienced in every season before that moment. You also might find yourself in that moment, like I did, wondering if following your heart and making the choice that was right for *you* was a blessing you deserved to have. You will wonder if all that you have fought for and said yes to could really be as marvelous and specifically for you as it feels. It was for me, and I hope that it will be for you too.

There may have been storm after storm in your Unfolding

◆

process thus far, and finally, *finally*, the sun has started to peek over the horizon. You're not quite "there" yet, wherever *there* is, but nonetheless you can experience a long-awaited and needed exhale, the deepest sigh, the reclaiming of your own clarity, and the only permission you need is the one you give yourself, time after time, to let the light in.

THIS YEAR COULD HAVE
broken you.
THIS YEAR COULD HAVE TAKEN
ALL THAT YOU HAVE
AND ALL THAT YOU ARE.
BUT HERE YOU ARE, BRUISED, STILL
standing, AND full.

SIGN

whatever it is that you're holding on to

that won't let you fully grow, heal, or step forward,

it's time to release it,

my love,

if you were looking for a sign,

this is it

AUDACITY

Sometimes *no* is the only way to release a *yes*
our tongues
find themselves unfamiliar in knowing
how to reach the roofs of our mouths
afraid of disappointing
afraid of not being included
unwilling to relinquish hold dates on our calendars
the tension of creating boundaries
but not boulders
but the very act of saying *no* will sometimes
be the only way to leave room for
gentleness for your own body and mind
to make room for more, for full cups
and love not in deficits but overflowing
practice the curve and art of *no* daily
rehearse the tip of your tongue
sounding out the two letters with graciousness
and subtle audacity
who are you who
decides to take care of yourself?
and may the only answer in return be,
how could I not?

MORE

Please don't stop dreaming
please don't stop pushing up ceilings
because that's exactly who dreamers are
and what we were made to do
people who don't believe
they will tell us
that we are crazy
but we're not,
we're just people who are used to breathing
in stars and knowing we were made for more

WILDFLOWERS

this is a letter for the wildflowers

who hear the music that no one else does

who dance to the rhythms of discomfort and uprooting

the wildflowers who choose

to rise from the dirt

and face the sun as if their lives depend on it

stretching themselves toward joy

no matter how knee-deep in the dirt they are

the wildflowers often mistaken for weeds

their beauty skipped over, unseen

and yet they still keep growing

with no permission needed

because they have come to terms with the reality

that they were not made for anyone else's approval,

they exist freely without human intervention

they grow where they want to

they go where they want to

they dance because they want to

wild with no apologies,

I wonder what the flowers think of us

I wonder if they'd whisper to us,

we know what you're really here for,

you want to escape,

you want to escape outside of yourself but there

has been just enough sunshine,

laced in between your bones,

made up of water and soul.

You are just as bold

and bright as we are,

the only difference is—

you don't live like you know it yet

NEVER FORGET

it's like shedding skin that no longer fits

it's unraveling an exhale of a breath

you've been holding for far too long

it's the letting go

being able to say,

this is who I was

but this is not who I am today

and that is okay

it's like standing, audaciously but humbly

leaving flowers on the shadows

of the woman you used to be

don't call it a funeral,

this here is a revival

Permission Slip

Repeat these affirmations to yourself today with an inhale before each phrase and an exhale after.

(Inhale)
I am a deep well of joy and infinite possibilities.
(Exhale)

(Inhale)
I am home to love and compassion for myself and others.
(Exhale)

(Inhale)
Today, I give myself permission to find peace in the little things.
(Exhale)

(Inhale)
Today I give myself permission to protect, nurture, and tend to the person I am and the person I'm becoming.
(Exhale)

Think about what you might need to give yourself permission to do or be today. Know that you are the only person who needs to ask this of you, and you have full freedom to respond with all the permission you need.
Today I give myself permission to

AS I STEP INTO THE PERSON

I am
becoming,

MAY I RETURN INFINITE

THANKS TO
THE PERSON **I was.**

BE KIND

Be kind to all the past versions of you,

they are the soil from which you now bloom.

give your past selves their flowers too,

do not be so quick to write them off,

they are the soil from which you now bloom

be kind in how you speak about them,

be gracious

over and over again

for each of you who will come to exist

NEED TO PLEASE

"You are not the person I thought you were,"
she said, disappointment heavy on a face I'd never seen
nor a voice I'd ever heard
I inhaled and responded,
"I am sorry that you created a perspective
and expectation of me that I don't meet"
and then I whispered a gentle apology to myself,
"I'm sorry that you believed that
you had to meet those expectations in the first place."

Free

Like a caged bird or chained lion, it is through the chain breaking or wing releasing that you begin the process of Unfolding and can move toward healing and freedom. It's a wonderful process to be in, but sometimes your freedom becomes a threat to others because it reminds them of their own chains. If you let other people's fear of your freedom hold you back, it creates a codependency to your old patterns and selves and keeps you from experiencing your fullness.

While moving through my Unfolding process, one of my fears was that I was going to "unravel" or "stray" so far away from God that I would wind up lost in the wilderness somewhere. But instead, what I felt in my spirit as I walked toward the unknown, as I paved a different path for myself and ventured into Awakening, Eclipsing, Illuminating, and Returning, was that I wasn't walking further away but was diving more deeply inward. I was releasing the fears that I had to keep God in a box where all that was said was "Don't touch that, or go there, or do that, or be there," and instead, I needed to allow the expansive and omnipresent existence to guide me into boundless waters.

What are the things that hold you back? What are the chains that keep you from being your fullest and most free self? Chains are not always literal. There are moments when we are bound to brokenness that doesn't belong to us—that is a chain. Sometimes we are distracted by who we think we *should* be and it keeps us from fully becoming who we are meant to be—that is also a chain.

◆

The chains holding me back during this time were chains that were not mine to carry: comparison, people pleasing, not wanting to disappoint family and friends, not trusting my own two feet, thinking that my mentors and teachers knew better than I knew myself. I carried chains that made me think if I lost my community, I couldn't gain another one who would see and love me for my fullness. Our greatest desire and our greatest fear is belonging. But what is belonging, what is a safe haven, what is a community that truly holds us if not one that holds *all* of us? Sometimes belonging can look like listening to expectations held over us and to break them means confronting our fear of not belonging, choosing to go against the grain in certain spaces. This fear can be debilitating, and that too is a chain. But if there's anything that a history of our country has shown us specifically it's that chains are meant to be broken, fullness is designed to be stepped into, and freedom . . . well, we have always been made for and deserving of freedom.

I AM NOT ashamed OF WHO I'VE BEEN.
I am not afraid OF WHERE I AM GOING.
AND I, WITH OPEN HAND, FULL HEART, accept
WHO I WILL BECOME.

BREATHE, RELEASE, UNFOLD

Why are you giving those outside voices so much power?
who are they to deserve
so much of your sanity,
your well-being, your energy?
why do you make room
for exhausting interactions
that fatigue your existence?
my love, my love
release, unfold
release and unfold
breathe
reclaim your power
protect your sanity,
reserve your energy
make room for what fills,
not for what empties

ALL OF US ARE TIRED

Are you tired yet?
feel free to take off everything you thought you had to be
feel free to take off the too big or too small shoes
you were made to believe you had to fit into
feel free to strip yourself of the
heavy expectations placed on your shoulders
release yourself from
the constricting views of others
let go of the thought you have
to do or be anything
to be enough
Are you tired yet?
it must be so exhausting to believe
that you have to be anything but
who you already are
to be enough

VALUE

I am learning how to
unwind the narrative
from my existence
that I am not enough
with every inhale,
I will be reminded of my worth
I will listen to every heartbeat
and know that my value has always been: priceless
and know that I have always been whole

SOME KIND OF MAGIC

There is a magic

nestled in the curves of hips

sitting in the corners of a smile

dancing every time a laugh escapes from her lips

A magic

that makes a home in mother, in daughter, in sister, in wife

There is a magic

that exudes from every woman I've ever known

filled with stories of

falling and rising

rising and falling but never staying there

carrying words that are buried underneath one too many

    I'm sorrys

we have started apologizing for the way our souls glisten

    in the sun

we have made excuses for the way our

strength holds up empires

tried to make sense of our

feeling and caring,

shoving it under sticks and stones

so that it would make us seem less weak

we have bit our tongues for too long

our silence mistaken for tolerance

but you see we—

we are the revolution that happens at night

when everyone else is sleeping

when eyes are closed and breathing is heavy and rhythmic

made with dust and a whole lot of glory

my goodness,

ain't I a woman

and ain't I some kind of magic

Mantra

Repeat after me:

It's okay to outgrow and unlearn
what I've known
to make room for wonder and mystery.
It's okay to outgrow and unlearn
what I've known
to make room for who I will become.

Thin Space

I told one of my spiritual mentors once that I had felt for a while as though I was watching someone else live my life. Or as if I was lying down in a coma state and my mind was active and aware yet my body was still and unmoving, while life and sounds and voices all existed around me. She looked at me and said, "You have the ability to do this . . ." Then, with her thumb and index finger pressed together, she began to rotate and flip them up and down. "You have the ability to shift between heaven and Earth. When it's said 'on Earth as it is in heaven,' the word 'in' is actually 'on.'" I stared at her for a moment and noticed the tears start to stream down my face.

After lots of conversations such as this, I realize now that what she was telling me about was the "thin space." It is indeed the Earth as it is in heaven because heaven has always been here. It is the space where the Holy meets the human. Where the rushing of a divine presence meets us here in the mundane. It is where a shifting of the atmosphere happens and begs us to lean in and take note. The thin space is home to the out-of-body moments in which sometimes what is being experienced takes a while to be felt.

We live in the thin space more often than we are consciously aware of.

In the thin space is where we experience goose bumps on our arms when something affects us so deeply that it tickles our soul, and our body can't help but respond. There we find a permission to return to our own voice, to the depth set inside of us ready to be beckoned and brought forth at any moment

possible, where heaven meets this flesh and these bones and encourages and reminds our soul of our belonging. Our belonging that has always, always been there.

Heaven is here.

Heaven is you.

Heaven is me.

Heaven is us.

Heaven is right now,

in the holding of grief and joy,

in the sifting of the mundane.

On Earth as it is in heaven,

may it be so.

INTERSECTION OF HOLY

You are free to meet Holy outside of four walls

free to dance with the Divine

as you bask in the sun,

learning to keep your eyes facing up

May your curiosity bring you back to faith

and may doubting cause you to step out onto waters

you did not know you could step out onto before

You are allowed to commune with grass

and the birds and the trees—do you hear the glory rising?

Where your breath is,

there the Light will meet you

The Illuminating is a space of revealing new perspectives, fresh eyes, and a new light. What can you see with this new perspective?

_____

What are the "chains" that you find yourself needing to break free from?

_____

What is holding you back from your final release, the next exhale?

_____

Where can you find the "light moments" in your life right now? Write them down to remember that there are still silver linings.

_____

What is a lesson that nature teaches you about yourself or the world around you?

_____

What is encompassed in your "thin space"? In what ways do you feel the most connected to something bigger than yourself?

_____

Today I give myself permission to:

Breathe, release, unfold.
Breathe, release, unfold.
Breathe, release, unfold.
Breathe, release, unfold.

The Returning

ou know that moment after a vacation, or even a really long day, when you return home? You kick off your shoes, you might take off your bra or that one item you couldn't wait to throw and let fall wherever it may. Home is a place to slip on something comfy, wash off the makeup, make a meal (or order takeout) that makes you dance a little, and settle into the folds of your couch that knows how to specifically hold you. Maybe it's not your own home but someone else's home that feels like your own, or a place in the park that you continue to return to, or maybe even your office space. That's The Returning. It's *that* feeling, that deep knowing that you are safe, seen, full, and whole. That you can be *all* of you there, whatever and whoever that may be at that moment. Returning to light and love, acknowledging it in yourself and those around you. Where you are covered in provision and abundance, everything you need is right here and everything you are can bloom here.

Take a moment to close your eyes and dwell in that feeling for a moment. If you're not physically in that place, then mentally escape there and take a deep breath as you do.

Beautiful, welcome back.

For me, The Returning was being reunited with my sanity. It meant I trusted myself again—my decisions, my discernment, my intuition. I began to understand how to lean into this spirit of knowing and discerning, living again in my gut, which has guided me thus far. I was returning to my voice. I wasn't doubting myself or what I wanted or my passions in that moment, wasn't letting the opinions of others sway me left and right or convince me of what I wanted or didn't want. I was also returning to my body, to trusting her too, believing that she was good, worthy, and that I did not have to confine myself in a stifling "good girl box" that would mean I couldn't experience freedom in my own skin. I spent too long not knowing what it meant to embrace fullness and freedom in my body, and I can't go back. If we, as Christians, claim to be so free in Christ, then why do we still have all these chains? So yeah, you can find me dancing like David . . . in my underwear, sipping wine. *Selah.*

The Returning means I can encounter God again in a way that isn't clouded with asking: *Is this God's voice, or the voice of an authority figure in my life?* I am going to be honest and say that these days, it's still pretty hard to pick up my Bible or dive into scriptures because I am still learning how to see them as talking with me rather than talking *at* me. I am relearning (slowly) how they serve as meditations, gentle reminders, leaving room for new realizations and awakenings, and how there is so much potential for healing in them. I have these beautiful coffee-table versions of different Gospels and books of the Bible from a company called Alabaster Co. Their mission is "for all of humanity to experience God as beautiful," to "bring forth beauty in the world,"[1] and because of their reviving of scripture in tangible and beautiful renditions, I find myself drawn to those reflections and parables of God's grace again.

The Returning means I find solace in not forcing myself to attend a Sunday service every week but instead let my Sabbath take many other forms of worship, like resting, being, watering my plants, washing my hair, finding communion with the sand and sea or allowing my yoga mat to give me all the sermon I may need for that day. When I do crave the community and the beauty of being around like-minded people, I attend New Abbey, a local church whose focus is shifting the narratives we've been raised with, as well as addressing the deconstruction and welcoming the reconstruction. I also realized that my heart for social justice was extensive and inclusive and needed to encompass those of the Black and brown communities as well as my LGBTQ+ loved ones and acquaintances. It was important to me to be in a community that I felt reflected what this deeply desired heaven could look like, and it is the most glorious piece of heaven I could experience on a Sunday morning.

---

1 "Our Story," Alabaster Creative, accessed June 3, 2022, https://www.alabasterco.com/pages/our-story.

In The Returning, I learned that my Blackness was not a separate entity from my spirit, from my spirituality or my faith, and after disassociating myself from a whitewashed Jesus that diminished Black identity, I made it part of my spiritual practice to connect with a theology that did not enforce injustices on others but instead liberated us. I would attend churches and visit communities that did not ignore the oppression of Black and brown bodies, from Black to Asian to Latinx and beyond, but encountered it head-on, hand in hand. And I gave myself the permission not to have to be a Black spokesperson for every bit of pain we may experience, but in any moment I could speak my truth as much as I could speak nothing and go and live a beautiful, Black, and joy-filled life without explanation or permission.

The Returning also gave me a freedom I didn't even know was possible. A freedom to live life in all its fullness and experience every bit of grief, joy, gratitude, Awakening, Eclipsing, Mending, and Illuminating in every opportunity. It meant I could be fully present and free in a marriage, a partnership, in which I was not less than but equal to. I had a voice just as much as my husband did, and I could speak into him with the same weight he could speak into me. The freedom also brought a lot of joy in being me and in John being fully himself too.

The Returning brings us back to the goodness that was always meant for us. We know the story of wrongdoings and catastrophe; we need more room for the stories of hope, the stories of peace, the stories about the goodness we were intended for. A return to the garden of freedom, of intimacy with our Creator and our naked body and soul. *Selah.*

◆

OUT OF HIDING

A friend came over one evening for dinner

I lit a candle

I vacuumed the carpet

fluffed the pillows

mopped the kitchen

the usual tidying

but I did not feel the need to hide

unwanted pieces in the closets,

mostly because they were already full to begin with

I did not tuck the dirty laundry into an unseen place

instead the pile sat where the pile has sat

The corner clutter of my office

stayed just as such

and what permission that is—

to not have to hide the unwanted pieces of who we are

to not tuck away under the bed the parts of us we find dirty

to let the clutter be clutter

and know that we are still wholeheartedly

and fully able to be embraced, loved, seen

come out of hiding, love,

pull from under the bed the pieces of you hiding

and come as you are

come as all that you are

Breathe

As you read these words,
I hope you take a moment to follow their guidance.

Inhale through your nose.
Exhale through your nose.

Inhale through your nose.
Exhale through your nose.

Remember this breath
that you have been given.
This breath reminds you that you are okay,
that you are not in danger,

that you are not falling apart.

Inhale through your nose.
Exhale through your nose.

Inhale through your nose.
Exhale through your nose.

Release any thought that you have to be anywhere
or do anything and just be present in this very moment.

Inhale through your nose.
Exhale through your nose.

Here begins the stilling of
self,
mind,
body.

Inhale through your nose.
Exhale through your nose.

Come back to your natural breath
and begin your day.

RETURN

Perhaps we do not find ourselves,

we simply release the lie

we needed to be anyone else,

we unfold from these boxes

and at last

return

NOSTALGIA

There is something so beautiful

about the fragility of our humanity

we were created to rest and remain

within a garden of goodness

of light and love

of provision and abundance

And then the heaviness and fullness of truth and chaos

came into existence and shifted

our very foundation of living fully

in our truest form

and thus

so much of our existence now

revolves around an attempt

to return to that light and love

provision and abundance

and to return

we must first sift through distractions,

decipher the noise of lies

from the whispers of truth

to bring ourselves

to the ultimate place of peace and rest

we must first thread ourselves

to the very essence of our existence

we must first dare to see bodies, flesh and bones,

souls and spirits, as breathing, beating,

beautiful beings

This is The Returning of self

the rejuvenation of human being

and not human doing

a returning to the light and love

within each and every one of us

the light and love surrounding

every person

every body

every spirit and soul

the essence of our existence

is the quieting of mind

is the stillness of body

and the return to being

the return to being

SACRED FEMININE

May I be so emboldened
that I remember the strength
of this spine inside of me
focused toward heaven,
remember not the fold of my breaking
but the rise of everyday victories
may I not cower at the uncertainty of approval from others
may I not live as though my existence
must be shaped by the applause
that was never meant to hold up these two feet
confidence
being the foundation worth standing on
not solid in certainty but fluid in existing
that the wonder of not having the answers
is a lighter weight to hold
than being trapped in certainty
may I release the need to be anything but present
anything but here tapped into this breath
this sticky, sweet, sweaty reminder of what a glorious wonder
it is to be alive, moving, breathing,
here with open hands and not clenched fists
I want to be in awe of the unknown
and enamored with even the greatest wonder in myself
and the glorious world around me

◆

to look at my flesh and be reminded of the Holy

to look at my tears

and think of the same weeping of the Divine

to look at these curves, breasts and crevices

and think of every mountain and valley

shaped by hands big enough to hold all of me too

what's the harm in seeing God in the image of women

how far off would it be for women to be from the

    Holy anyway

HOME

home does not always change
sometimes it serves as a constant reminder
of how we have changed
when we step on the same floorboards as always
and yet our feet,
more aware of their weight, settle differently
there is now a creak that sings underneath your presence
that was not there before
The curtains, unchanged, still framing the same window
but the light, slipping through, bounces off your skin
in ways that cause you to watch the light
and your skin to learn a new dance
Sometimes
the voices in the rooms will remind you of your shifting
will tell you how loud your steps are,
will tell you it's much too bright inside,
that you must shut the curtains
the walls will feel as though they are closing in
perhaps this is what Maya Angelou
meant by the caged bird
perhaps expansion and growth
are all about realizing your wingspan
home, the same space, the same four walls
reminding us of our own shifting

every single time we return

showing us

the new weight underneath our steps

the new light dancing off of our skin

showing us the span of our wings,

home does not always change

sometimes it is simply the moment of connection

showing us the arc in our story

the rise of our spine

and the stretch of our span

the new weight in our feet

giving the urge to close the door

of the walls that grew us

and find a new home,

one that does not creak underneath your ponderous steps

one where the light always dances

on your skin and your wings

There are no four walls to tell your body, your heart,

your soul, your feelings

how wide they can stretch any longer

this new home,

reminding you to release and expand

release and expand

and return home to yourself time and time again

I HAVE FOUGHT
TO STRETCH MY WINGS
THIS FAR.
I will not shrink
FOR THOSE
WHO CANNOT
TAKE THE WHOLE OF ME.

VOICE

As a teenager, I didn't talk much
I grew up uncomfortable in my own skin
hiding behind a body that didn't feel like my own
A body that felt massive and unlovable
I stayed on the outside of social circles,
kept to myself because I was still
learning how to be myself
and then one day I found my voice
that shaky, unfamiliar existence
that I shoved deep down inside
because of the lies in my own head
repeating themselves like a lullaby
that always convinced me that I was not enough
the shoveling weight that tried to
bury my worthiness
but I climbed from under its hold
before it could take my breath
and from that point, I made it my mission,
that whatever I did in this world
I would remind every woman,
every person I encountered
that there is a certain magic in their bones
and I may not know you,

I may not have ever heard your voice

but I bet it sounds the way it would

if mountains came crashing into a sea:

powerful and unstoppable

I bet that your mind is a mosaic, easy to get lost in

and swimming with brilliance

and I'm sure that I could count the times

that you've looked at yourself in the mirror

and compared your body to someone else's

but, darling, the beauty you possess only belongs to

    you and no one else

the story that you are weaving belongs to you and

    no one else

and no one can tell it quite like you

So this is the moment

this is the moment when you dare to get up

shake off the fear, shake off the doubt

dance your hardest

listen to the music your very feet orchestrate

and when you've found the tune

grab someone else's hand and sing it to them too

because the most powerful thing you can do,

when you finally know who you truly are,

is to remind someone else who they are too

to look someone in the eye and say

"You are enough
You are enough
and you are needed here"
I'll go first and I'll say it to you
"You are enough
and you are needed here"

FEELER

I am a sensitive soul

I feel in waves

I feel in oceans

I feel everything at once

I have always been a feeler

I have always carried bricks

meant for everyone else's

homes on these shoulders

and assumed that it was

how it was meant to be

I am walking journal pages

that should be tucked deep

into boxes and shoved under beds

always spilling, always bleeding

I am a carrier of hurt

a ship never meant to find shore

always sailing

always filling more than her capacity to hold

Do not be afraid to feel

do not be afraid to be a bleeding heart

you are not too sensitive

you are not emotional

you are human

deeply,

feeling human

WELCOME HOME

Imagine how freeing it is,

to come home to your own body

and no longer have bags to unpack

no more overflowing boxes left in the corners

no more skeletons in the closet

the shoes are off

the boxes are away

the blinds are open

the candle is lit

welcome

home

MINIMALIST

I have learned to love dancing naked

I have decided that a bra is much too stifling

whoever told us those were a good idea to begin with?

I have understood how to let go of expectations of me

that were not my own to meet

I spring clean my mind

every time it gets too loud

I am beginning to love the walls of my office

with fewer photos on them

finding beauty in the less

by no means will I ever be a minimalist

but I have found a love for less

less shame

less hiding

less guilt

more room for naked dance

and bare shaking

for a lighter load

for kisses that linger gently

for the simpler things

like a stripped-from-judgment type of soul

like a body who moves like it remembers

it was always made for more

There You Have Always Been

Here's where the misconception of change begins: we wake up one day and look in the mirror and notice someone different and yet strikingly familiar all at once. It's not like all of sudden we become confident. We didn't snap our fingers and find our beliefs had changed and expanded. The roaring lioness in our chest did not just suddenly appear. The confidence built over months and years engrained and embodied itself in our spines so that, over time, we learned to stand a little taller, tall enough for our crowns to stop sliding off. Our faces dance in the sun's rays again, like we were created from the beginning. The growth has been steadily happening to The Unfolding occurring gently while we slept, while we cried, while we prayed. The undoing, the relearning, has created a foundation stronger than before.

And the lioness? Well, the lioness has always been there.

She just waited patiently for us to claim her as our own. To hear the roaring in our chest and not automatically assume it was outside of us but *in us*, part of us.

When people say "I don't recognize you" or "I don't know who you are anymore," these are no longer negative statements. They are testaments and reminders: keep growing, keep unraveling and unfolding. Because while the voices may be trying to convince you that who you are becoming is not who you should be, you will look back at the reflection in the mirror and find it is no longer an unfamiliar face. Instead it is a breath, an exhale of remembrance, an acknowledgment and release: *Oh, there you are. And there you have always been.*

◆

ALWAYS BEEN

Before a butterfly becomes a butterfly
before its beauty is broadcasted
it is a small form of itself
a caterpillar that moves slowly on its belly,
shuffles through life
and then comes the transforming,
then comes the space where the struggle
and the push and the pull feels like a never-ending season
It is a space that feels like breaking
but in reality it is only the shaping
the moment when the tension comes pressing in
the butterfly comes exhaling out of its cocoon
the moment the dust settles
wrestling turns into stillness
the hiding comes before the blooming
and even with eyes closed you can still bask in the sun
bathe in the light, absorb the light,
become the light, walk in the light,
show the light,
know that all this darkness is not in vain
a shadow is only a shadow
until it is all light
like it's always been
like you've always been

GOD IS THERE

They told me there was no Holy in my doubting
but I would say that it was my questions that broke the
    clouds open
and zeal fell like rain
and, on Earth as it is in heaven, found itself in my lungs
they said that I was off-roading but instead
I heard God's whisper in the wilderness and decided to
    follow it
they told me God was not in the whimsy
and yet I noticed the holy presence most
when I peeled my body off of pews
and was thrown into the unknown
so this is sermon, so this is worship
so this is the God-breathed life into dry bones
that we have been searching for
Now in the wind, I know God is there
now in the dance of the waves, I know God is there
now as I stand, human and messy
and still loved, goodness etched in my form,
God is there

WILD THING

We only call things wild and crazy
when they do not conform
to patterns of existing
for the sake of being palpable or comfortable
We have become accustomed
to taming wild things,
painting the act as a form of rescue
and not calling it what it is: conditioning
The leashed dog runs outside
of its boundaries and colonizing
the caged lion knows it was made for more
A woman learns to trust her instincts
and follow the Divine leading
that has always been inside of her
all this talk of wild and crazy
perhaps is just unlearning, nonconforming
Shedding layers of conditioning
and embracing finally
this wild was never something to be afraid of,
it was always the thread back home to ourselves
and connection to something so
much
bigger
than all of it

LOST

You are only lost

if there is a destination

you cannot reach

and even then,

there is still something beautiful

about the wander

So maybe there is a destination after all

and maybe you're not lost—

perhaps we're all just wanderers,

all finding a way back to ourselves

only to find that we were truly returning

to one another

THE SAME SONG

I once saw an art exhibit at The Broad
called *The Visitors*
in it, screens showed twelve different artists
all singing the same song,
each playing different instruments,
their voices all melting together
creating the most beautiful echo
their voices rising into
a marvelous catastrophe of sound
colliding together in the center of the room
as slowly each screen began to empty,
the sound began to fade,
and I watched them enter into the same room
their feet bare, a piano playing, their guitars strumming
each of their ballads
tiptoeing around each other
watching this,
I wondered if humanity could be like this one day
if we could all be singing
the same song in different rooms
but find our differences would not be so different after all
if we listened closely,
would we find that the melody
has always been the same

would we find that the blood

running through our veins

has always flowed the same

if we remember that the breath in our lungs

has sometimes carried the same rhythm at one time

I wonder if we stripped down this skin,

would we find that our bones

are all the same color

that our insides all bleed red

and pulse alive

if we realized after all this time

we never knew we were singing the same song

in the same house

just in different rooms

I wonder what would happen

if we turned the lights on,

if we would finally see each other

finally hear that the melody

has been the same

all along

FINALLY

"I have finally arrived"
she whispered

where?
"back home to myself."

STILL THERE

I haven't lost you,
for you are closer than my breath
where can I go to find you?
anywhere, anywhere
if you are a God of everything
then you are a God who sees me
You see me

SVADHYAYA (SELF-STUDY)

The trees do not pray to be with God

the river does not ask to be close to the Divine

the stars do not ask for the right way to be near the Holy

They do not have to

because they are fully aware

they are always with God

they are always close to the Divine

they are always near the Holy

we ask God, *"Who are you?"*

God says, *"I am."*

we ask God, *"Who am I?"*

to which God says with no delay,

"You are."

Yoga Mat

One Sunday I woke up, rolled out my yoga mat to stretch and move my body to begin my day. As I was doing so, I put some "soaking worship music" on YouTube, grabbed my foam roller, and as I lay there, stretching out the tension and discomfort in my back, I began to sing, *"I haven't lost you . . . for you are closer than my breath. I haven't lost you . . . for you are closer than my breath. Where can I go to find you? Anywhere . . . anywhere."* As the words began to spill out of me, I began to weep, still singing. Finally the last phrase met me in my moment: *"If you are a God of everything, then you are a God who sees me. . . . You see me."* Sometimes in my most raw and open moments, I get what I call "spillings." Sometimes those spillings are poems and sometimes they are melodies. It is always such a euphoric moment when I receive these words or melodies, because before I share them with others, they are first love letters to myself. And goodness, did I need that one in that moment.

When we assess the moments in our lives that could have been divinely orchestrated, we start to see a pattern of simplicity. We have complicated the process of meeting The One, who surrounds us every day. Closer than our very breath, God breathed: us. Walking light bearers and image carriers, how can we be distant from something that we *are*? Deeply connected and beautifully surrounded.

This is not the first time I have wept and worshipped on a yoga mat. In fact, this occurrence has happened many times over the past few years of regularly practicing yoga. It has become one of the most tender, vulnerable, and exposing places where time and time again I have met myself with grace and intimacy and I have found the grace and covering of God all at the same time.

Perhaps you find yourself in places you never thought you would. Maybe you are unraveling the sacredness and divineness of your existence in the most mundane or simple of places and maybe that's where you will find God too.

Today I Exist

For this body meditation, I encourage you to find
a settled position either sitting or lying down.
As you do this, gently notice where you may be
holding on to tension in your body and, as kindly
as possible, send your breath to those parts of
your body. Take note of your natural inhales
and exhales.

If you feel safe doing so, place a hand over your
heart and your other hand over your stomach.
Again, take note of your natural inhales and exhales.
As you breathe, send love to each part of you,
from your head to your toes.

Today you exist.
Today you are full of life.
Today there is breath in your lungs.
There is blood in your veins.
There is life inside of you.

Today I exist.
Today I am full of life.
Today there is breath in my lungs.
There is blood in my veins.
There is life inside of me.

There is life in your fingertips.
There is life in your toes.
There is life inside of you.

There is life in my fingertips.
There is life in my toes.
There is life inside of me.

This life that has been placed within your existence
is one made to be full:
Full of joy.
Full of grief.
Full of experience.
Full of love.
Full of laughter.
Full of pain and sometimes suffering.

You have been given life.
You have been put here for a reason.
You are not a mistake.
You are not an accident.
You exist on purpose.
You were made for a purpose and with purpose.

I have been given life.
I have been put here for a reason.
I am not a mistake.
I am not an accident.
I exist on purpose.
I was made for a purpose and with purpose.

You were made with
orchestration, with intention,

life breathed into existence,
and the making of your very being
was considered very good.

Today you exist.
Inhale the existence of today
and exhale what was yesterday.

Today deserves its own intention
and awareness.

You are alive today.
You exist in right now,
present within your own body,
connected with your own spirit and soul.
Allow them to meet, allow them to breathe as one.

Connect your breath with the synchrony of the
life pumping in your veins.
Remember that the breath in your lungs is your
greatest advocate.
Take note of the life in every exhale.

GRAND RISING

did you rise today with gratitude in your bones?

did you gently squeeze all the beautiful,

squishy parts of you and say, *"Thank you for being here"*?

did you breathe deep and think what a gift this is?

so, love, did you wake up today with gratitude in your bones?

THE ART OF LOVING YOURSELF (PART 3)

Throw a party, just for you.

Buy your favorite snacks (do not count the calories),

put your favorite flowers in a vase.

Invite all the parts of you that you wish to hide,

learn to celebrate all of them

throw confetti, just because.

Play your favorite song,

dance barefoot.

exhale.

repeat.

this is what it means to finally be free.

DECLARATION OF THE SEA

And the ocean always reminds me

that I was made for deep waters

that surface living

is the most drowning of them all

so give me a life that takes my breath away

give me horizons that keep me in awe

of their appearance of infinity

let the waves remind me

of every dip and curve

worth loving on my own body

the crashing of waves

matching my heartbeat

the sand shows me that it's okay

not to be for everyone,

only some are willing to

tread in the uncomfortable

let the ocean sing the anthem of audacity:

"I change for no one," it declares,

"I change for no one."

THE PRESENT JOURNEY

When you first began the journey
no one told you how much to pack
what to prepare for when you got there
or how long it would take you to get there
in fact no one really told you the destination at all,
where is *there* anyway?
you just know that you're supposed to go
When you first began,
your heart was full of excitement
your hands uncalloused
and eager to work
When you first began,
nothing could stop you
no one could stop you
and now, sometimes it feels as though
anything could try and stop you
and sometimes seems to succeed
your suitcase feels heavier
than when you first began
and you have more baggage
than you would like to admit
the arrival,
the arrival will be worth it,

eventually,

whenever it happens

if it happens

but the journey,

the journey

will be where the stories are

where you grow the most

where you find your strength

where your bravery will bloom

and your courage soar

where your understanding of your worth

will become dangerously clear

and no one can tell you otherwise

most days, you will have more questions

than you will have answers

and you won't be certain of very much

but one thing you can be certain of is

that where you are right now

is exactly where you should be

see, it's not about where we are going

it's about how we are getting there

it's about every small beginning

it's about how we ignore fear

and decide to take the first leap

it's about how we are *still* afraid

and yet we do it anyway

so embrace the journey

the present journey

we are not done yet,

you are not done yet

for it is only the most beautiful beginning

KNOW THAT EVEN DEEP BREATHS
CAN BE CONSIDERED SLOW STEPS

forward.

SO WHEN IT FEELS LIKE
YOU'RE NOT MOVING,
REMEMBER
YOU'RE STILL BREATHING,
AND THAT IS MORE THAN ENOUGH.

Say Yes

On May 23, 2021, John and I celebrated our one-year anniversary. I often think back over this first year in awe of how much we overcame to say yes to this love we have. I look at him sleeping—his silhouette is one of the most beautiful sights to me. I feel his warm arm around my waist and his gentle kisses, and I think about how I almost was too afraid to say yes to all of this. I think about how I almost let this taunting, testing version of what I understood God to be keep me from seeing the goodness of the Divine, in all its kindness and love. I think about how I spent months not knowing fully who I was anymore, weighted down by the voices and opinions of others so much so that I couldn't even recognize my own.

Thanks to a mentor and dear friend of ours, we recently learned that "perfect" doesn't mean flawless or blemishless. One definition, when I looked up "perfect," is actually "having all the required or desirable elements, qualities, or characteristics; as good as it is possible to be." *As good as it is possible to be.* Which means I can earnestly say that life in this moment, even as I've moved through Awakening and Eclipsing, even amongst The Illuminating and The Returning, is perfect. I think back to the shaping of these last few years and I am grateful for their chiseling, challenging, and molding. The years did not reveal a new person; instead, they simply unfolded the person I was always meant to become. Life is not without problems, our relationship is not without flaws, but everything in this very moment is as perfect as it's meant to be.

◆

May you too find the courage to say yes to The Unfolding of your own identity, stories, and life journey. May you find that there is perfection and glorious opportunities in *everything* even if it takes a little longer to see them. May you embrace every phase and season as they arise. May you lean into the shaping and gently remind yourself that you are not breaking or drowning; you, my love, are unfolding and returning to you, the fullness of you and all that entails. My goodness, what a wonder.

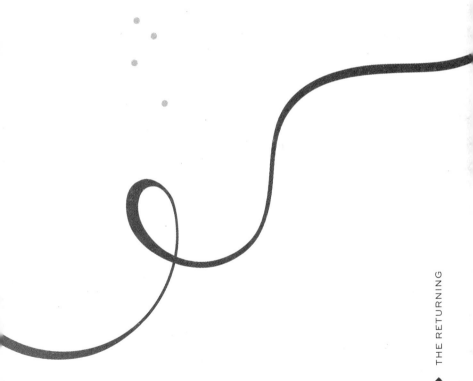

LOVE STORY

Find a love that brings out the stars in you,

shows you your light when you've forgotten what you're

   made of

a love that'll lasso the moon without saying a word,

just to remind you that they'll go to the ends of the Earth

to show you that no dream of yours is too big

find a love that makes you blink twice,

pinch yourself for a moment

just to see if this is a dream

and it's not too good to be true if it's meant for you,

if it tends to your soil while you learn how to bloom

if it shows you all the light and love you're made of

sings the light back into you in kisses when you forget

find a love that won't take you in pieces,

holds you whole

but not too tightly that you can't bloom again and again

find a love that brings out the stars in you

just to show you what you're made of

GLORIOUS

I have grown familiar

with the feeling of

holding out my hands

with the expectation

that I will pull them away empty

that a catastrophe would be made in every moment,

that instead of shooting stars,

atomic bombs will end up falling

so afraid that a solar eclipse

automatically implies there will be only darkness

and I will not notice that the light always returns

I have this bad habit of believing

that all good things that happen to me

are not actually for me

that somehow they dodged

the person they were meant for

and wound up in my lap by happenstance

I once attended a retreat

where they asked us if the glass was half full or half empty

and I said, *"Both,"* but it doesn't matter

because it's not my glass to begin with

I told them that even though glorious opportunities have

    happened to me,

they did not have my name on them

someone else dropped them

and I just so happened to be the next one

to pass by and picked them up

I was asked,

"So what does that mean you need to learn to accept?"

I said,

"I guess it means I need to believe

that I am deserving

of glorious opportunities."

"'I am deserving of glorious opportunities.'"

I am deserving of glorious opportunities.

"Now say it with your hands out,

like you're receiving."

I stood there with my hands open

and tears falling down my face

see, I am fully aware of the fact that

I am human and flawed

that the mediocrity of my humanity

often shadows

the still hint of sparkle in my dust

It often blocks the fact

that I am human and grace filled

and swimming with purpose

that there is nothing happenstance

about my existence or the things that happen to me

that my story is weaved with intention

even when I think it is not

I want to expect more shooting stars

than atomic bombs these days

and be in awe of the change that comes

after a solar eclipse

and learn to sit in the darkness when it arrives

take in the moment,

wear it like the warmest blanket I've ever worn

and then find the light again

because the light will always be there

I want to look at the glass and

know that no matter how much is inside of it,

its purpose is to hold things

so it doesn't matter if it's half full

or half empty

it is simply doing what it was made to do.

I want to hold out my hands

grasp the glorious parts of life

as if I were holding on to raindrops

watch them bounce on my palms

and still find them marvelous

even when they disappear

because even if they aren't mine to hold forever

at some point—no matter how long ago

they were still mine and they were glorious

Who are you? Without the weight of expectations
of others, who are you? This is the person you
are returning to.

What glorious opportunities are in your life right now?
Write them down so that you recognize how much
there is to be grateful for, and extend gratitude to them.

What would it look like to exist fully, intentionally,
and be in tune with your own body? How might
you put that into practice?

What parts of you do you wish to return to?
Name them and begin to make a daily habit of
embracing those parts of you more each day.

LIVE A BEAUTIFUL FREAKING LIFE,
WHATEVER THAT MEANS FOR YOU.

Dance wild.

MAKE YOUR OWN MUSIC.

DO NOT BE AFRAID OF BARENESS,

of flesh, of mind or soul,

BUT KNOW THAT NOT EVERYONE
IS DESERVING OF THE

NUDE VERSIONS OF YOU.

Love and
be loved.

YOU ARE DESERVING OF SUCH THINGS.

Acknowledgments

There is no forward motion without the cloud of witnesses who have guided us thus far. Though I have paved my way in a different direction, I am not the first to trek the path in which I now step and I am thankful for those who have unfolded and cleared the way before me.

To my parents, who have shaped me into the lioness, the woman I am today. Thank you for your commitment to loving and providing for us. Thank you for sacrificing all that you have to make sure we lived our best God-given lives. Thanks for the talents too (you know which one of you they're from) . . . Just kidding, Dad. I got your gift of gab too.

To my sisters, my lifelines and my favorite humans. I love you forever and always. No matter how far I travel or how far away I live, my heart is always with you.

To my granny, whom I feel I am a generational embodiment of, I remember very vividly talking about how you saw yourself on stages and creating magic too, and if you can't do it the way you imagined yourself doing it, then I hope I can do it for you.

To all the families that I have had the honor and privilege of choosing. We may not share blood, but you have no idea how much each and every one of you means to me. Each of you have mentored and guided, have loved and encouraged, have continued the shaping my parents began, and I am who I am today because of you too.

To Christine Suh, my dear, dear friend and the first person besides my editors to read the fourth draft of this book. Thank you for always seeing me, for holding me closely, and for speaking love and kindness and the words of our Creator over me time and time again. *Gamsahabnida.*

To Glennon Doyle. Your book *Untamed* came at the moment where I thought I was breaking and going insane; you reminded me I wasn't, that I was a goddamn cheetah realizing her caging and doing what it took to get free. Your words are a gift I cherish every day—thank you.

To my literary team, who has walked with me through this process. To Whitney, my agent, who was the first person to tell 2019 Arielle that she didn't have to write a book just because the opportunities were there to do so. Thank you for seeing me and caring for my craft so well.

To all of you who pick up this book, who give it to a friend, who read it and cherish it, thank you, thank you, thank you. Though I may not ever meet you face-to-face, know that the moment you touched this book, we became that much closer.

To my husband, my life partner, the person I truly cannot get enough of, John Corfee. Thank you for making space for the

◆

fullness of who I am. Thank you for giving me space to laugh and to cry and to throw fits and to spiral into my moments of doubt about who I am and what I'm capable of and reminding me of the truth. Thank you for your constant support and encouragement. You are my best yes and my embodiment of home. I love you with my whole heart and all of my being. By the way, have you seen the moon?